Hoyer Millar

Florida, South Carolina and Canadian phosphates

Giving a complete account of their occurrence, methods and cost of production

Hoyer Millar

Florida, South Carolina and Canadian phosphates
Giving a complete account of their occurrence, methods and cost of production

ISBN/EAN: 9783337113728

Printed in Europe, USA, Canada, Australia, Japan

Cover: Foto ©Suzi / pixelio.de

More available books at **www.hansebooks.com**

FLORIDA, SOUTH CAROLINA,

AND

CANADIAN PHOSPHATES:

GIVING A COMPLETE ACCOUNT OF THEIR OCCURRENCE,
METHODS AND COST OF PRODUCTION, QUANTITIES
RAISED, AND COMMERCIAL IMPORTANCE.

C. C. HOYER MILLAR.

LONDON:
EDEN FISHER & CO., 50, LOMBARD STREET, E.C.
MDCCXCII.

LONDON:

PRINTED BY EDEN FISHER & CO., 96-97, FENCHURCH STREET,

AND

50, LOMBARD STREET, E.C.

———

1892.

PREFACE.

———◆———

ALTHOUGH there is an abundance of literature upon the subject of the geological formation and chemical analysis of the various phosphates which have hitherto been discovered, yet it appears to me that the practical, though possibly sordid, side of the question has been rather neglected. Since, however, the phosphate mining industry is being carried on with the primary intention and hope of obtaining satisfactory returns from a pecuniary rather than a scientific point of view, I have ventured to give in the following pages an account, from a practical standpoint, of my personal investigations during the past few years in the phosphate fields of Florida, South Carolina and Canada. This book is therefore addressed to those who are commercially interested in phosphates, and should it be the means of giving them fuller information than they would be likely to gather elsewhere, then my efforts will be amply rewarded.

C. C. HOYER MILLAR.

1, FENCHURCH AVENUE, LONDON, E.C.
February 28th, 1892.

INDEX.

———◆———

CHAPTER I.—INTRODUCTORY.

CHAPTER II.—FLORIDA PHOSPHATES.

CHAPTER I.

INTRODUCTORY.

INTRODUCTION.

The tissues of every kind of vegetation are composed of a number of elements derived from the air, from water and from the soil. Those elements, therefore, of which the earth is deprived by agriculture, and which are not replaced by the action of air and water, have to be restored artificially if the life-supporting powers of the soil are to be kept in operation. Chief among these elements are nitrogen, potassium and phosphorus, the last-named being the most indispensable for the development of all plant and vegetable life.

Phosphorus is one of the most universally distributed of all elements ; it is found in every kind of animal and vegetable matter, as well as in most sedimentary and eruptive rocks, and existed previously to the dawn of life.

The necessity of re-stimulating an exhausted soil was discovered in very ancient times, but it is only during the present century that any real knowledge of cause and effect was acquired.

History shows that the excrement of birds was in use among the Romans, and that in the 12th century the Arabians and Peruvians used the guanos of their respective countries for fertilising purposes.

The waste clippings of bone and ivory from the button and knife factories of Sheffield (England) were utilised as a manure by the neighbouring farmers about the middle of last century, and this was probably the first occasion when any non-nitrogenous phosphatic material was thus employed. Towards the end of the century greensand was used in considerable quantities in the counties of Essex and Kent, and in the early part of the present century bones were so greatly in demand for application to the soil in a crushed form, that large imports were made from foreign countries in addition to the home collections.

About this same period the marl beds of New Jersey, U.S.A., were beginning to be exploited, and their contents used for enriching the agricultural lands of that State.

In France spent animal charcoal (bone black) began to be used as a manure in 1822, and the results were so satisfactory that its employment for agricultural purposes soon made rapid strides.

All this time the real cause of the stimulating effect of these various materials seems to have remained unknown, although the results were thoroughly recognised and appreciated.

It was apparently the French agricultural scientists who were the first to attribute to the phosphoric acid contained in the spent animal charcoal the beneficial effects resulting from the application of this material to the soil, and suggestions were made that the phosphates, discovered by Monsieur Berthier and others about the year 1820, should be mixed with the animal charcoal and crushed bones, and in 1841 a patent was taken out for the application of phosphates for agricultural purposes.

In the year 1840 Dr. Justus von Liebig, of Germany, who based his experiments on the researches of his predecessors, suggested the addition of sulphuric acid to crushed bones in order to render soluble the phosphate they contained. The phosphate of lime in bones had hitherto been considered useless owing to its being insoluble, and the fertilising element was thought to be in the gelatine matter ; in fact it was not until the Duke of Richmond proved by his experiments in the year 1843, that bones deprived of their grease and gelatinous matter were equally as efficacious as fresh bones, that the phosphoric acid was recognised as being the valuable fertilising element.

Meanwhile Mr. J. B. Lawes (now Sir J. B. Lawes) put Dr. Liebig's suggestions into practical effect, and began the manufacture of artificial manures at Deptford, London, by mixing sulphuric acid with the crushed bones. Soon afterwards (1845) Professor Henslow recommended Cambridge coprolites[*] (the analysis of which had been published by Monsieur Berthier, about the year 1820) as being a material rich enough in phosphate of lime to be a suitable substitute for bones, and the various bone-crushing factories were quickly converted into chemical fertiliser and superphosphate manufactories.

IMPORTANCE OF PHOSPHORIC ACID.

In order to show the great importance of phosphoric acid in relation to agriculture it may be mentioned that one year's crop in France—according to Monsieur Grandeau's recent estimation—removes from the soil about 300,000 tons of phosphoric acid, of which about one-half only is restored in the shape of stable manure.

In like manner it is estimated that the crop of wheat, maize, oats, barley, rye, buckwheat, hay and straw in the United States means an annual loss to the soil of nearly one and a-half million tons of phosphoric acid.

Further it has been shown that for every cow kept on pasture lands throughout the summer, there are carried off not less than 50 pounds of phosphate of lime in the shape of veal, cheese and butter.

---

[*] Note.—Professor Henslow named these nodules "coprolites," thinking that they were of coprolitic origin, like the nodules found in the Lias formation. He soon discovered his error, but the name (which is most misleading, since real coprolites are of very rare occurrence) has never been altered.

These few instances are sufficiently striking to show the enormous annual loss of phosphoric acid that is going on in all agricultural districts, and to prove the necessity for restoring to the soil what is being thus carried off.

SOURCES OF SUPPLY OF PHOSPHORIC ACID.

By a curious coincidence the discoveries of Dr. Liebig were published in the same year that the first few barrels of Peruvian guano were imported into England. This new fertiliser, which contained nitrogen in addition to phosphate, became at once so popular with the farmers that in the year 1845 the imports amounted to 283,000 tons, and by the year 1861 no less than 3,200,000 tons had been imported into the United Kingdom. The success of this guano resulted in the discovery of other guano deposits in the Pacific, on the east coast of South America, in the West Indies, in South Africa and in the Arabian Gulf. Of these only the Ichaboe, Patagonian and Falkland guanos were nitrogenous, the other deposits being purely phosphatic. Of the many guano deposits discovered nearly all have been exhausted, and at the present date the supply of this material is but small.

Bones, bone ash and bone meal continue to be a source of supply of phosphoric acid, but the quantities available form but a small proportion of the amount of phosphoric acid required annually.

The use of mineral phosphates* on the other hand has shown an enormous expansion since the early days when its manufacture was first begun, and deposits have been worked from time to time in the following countries :—Norway, Russia, Germany, England, Belgium, France, Spain, Algeria, Canada, United States (South Carolina and Florida), and many of the West Indian Islands, and also in Mexico and Brazil.

In addition to the above a fresh source of supply of phosphoric acid in the shape of ground basic slag was introduced into the European market about six years ago, and this material has given such satisfactory results that the annual consumption exceeds six hundred thousand tons.

These are the most important sources whence phosphoric acid is obtained, but there are also various waste and other products which supply smaller quantities.

THE PHOSPHATE MINING INDUSTRY.

Although Cambridge coprolites began to be worked as early as the year 1845, and used for the manufacture of chemical fertilisers, yet it was not till about the year 1870 that the phosphate mining industry began to assume any regularity or importance.

---

* Note.—The term "mineral phosphates" is used in the commercial sense, as contrasted with organic phosphates, such as bones, bone ash and soluble guanos.

This was doubtless owing to the immense supplies of guanos which were shipped in large quantities up to the year 1870,* soon after which date the best deposits became exhausted.

In the meantime the supplies of Cambridge coprolites had been supplemented by the working of similar beds in Suffolk and Bedfordshire.

In France the phosphates at Grandpré, in the Ardennes, began to be exploited in 1856, and applied to the soil in a ground state. Further discoveries were made at Quercy, in the department of Lot, in 1865, followed by the working in 1870 of the deposits of Lot-et-Garonne, Tarn-et-Garonne and Aveyron, known commercially as Bordeaux phosphates. A few years later the Boulogne coprolite deposits began to be exploited and shipments made to the United Kingdom.

In Spain, phosphate mining commenced on a small scale at Logrosan, in the province of Estramadura, about the year 1855, followed by mining near Caceres in 1860, where an output averaging 10,000 tons per annum was made up to 1875 from one mine alone.

In Norway, phosphates were discovered at Krageroe in 1854, and mining carried on for five years, during which time 13,000 tons were extracted and shipped. The Oedegärden deposits were not worked until after 1874.

*Note.—10,000,000 tons had been exported from the Chincha Islands alone.

In Germany, the Nassau phosphate deposits were discovered in 1864 : mining was at once commenced, and the phosphate exported, and also manufactured locally. Owing to the competition from other countries in recent years, and the high percentage of iron and alumina contained in these Lahn phosphates, their export ceased some years ago, and the whole production is now manufactured locally. From 20,000 to 30,000 tons are raised annually.

Phosphate deposits had also been opened in these years on some of the West Indian Islands, the most important sources being Navassa and Sombrero* Islands, from which places considerable quantities were shipped both to the United States and the United Kingdom.

In 1867 the South Carolina deposits began to be worked, and in four years' time the annual production of land and river rock had reached 65,000 tons.

The next ten years showed a great advance in the production of phosphates. Belgium entered the arena in 1873 with phosphates from the neighbourhood of Mons, and France began to supply larger quantities, 20,000 tons per annum being exported from the Bordeaux district alone. In 1875 the Ardennes and Meuse productions reached the figures of 25,000 and 41,000 tons respectively. In 1877, France produced a total quantity of 115,000 tons.

---

*NOTE. The island of Sombrero has been worked for over 30 years, and has produced a total quantity of 500,000 tons of uniformly high-grade phosphate.

In the West Indies the Islands of Curaçao and Aruba were now supplementing the output of high-testing phosphates, and the shipments from these sources in 1880 amounted to over 10,000 tons.

Spain was now producing and exporting larger quantities, 33,000 tons being shipped to the United Kingdom in 1874, 11,000 tons in 1879 and 23,000 tons in 1880.

The world's production of phosphates in 1880 appears to have been about as follows :—

	Tons.
England (Cambridge, Bedford and Suffolk coprolites)	30,000
France (Ardennes, Meuse, Lot, Tarn-et-Garonne, Aveyron, Boulogne, &c.)	125,000
Belgium (Mons District)	15,000
Spain (Estramadura)	40,000
Germany (Lahn District)	25,000
Norway	5,000
Canada..	7,500
South Carolina (Land Rock)	125,000
Do. (River Rock)	62,000
Curaçao, Aruba, and Sombrero Islands	10,000
Other West Indian Islands, Navassa, &c.	25,000
Other Countries	30,000
	500,000

In the next ten years the sources of supply altered very considerably. Spain, which in the years 1882 and 1883 shipped a quantity of 100,000 tons to the United Kingdom alone, has now practically ceased to export.

In France the old sources of supply for export have been replaced by the newer fields in the Somme and other northern departments.

Belgium has assumed an important place in the market, about 150,000 tons per annum being raised in the neighbourhood of Mons, while fresh deposits of large extent have recently been discovered and worked near Liège.

The South Carolina deposits have been developed to an enormous extent, consequent on the expansion of the chemical fertiliser manufacturing industry in the United States, and a new field has begun to be exploited in Florida.

In 1890 the production of phosphates had reached the following figures :—

		Tons.
England (Coprolites)	about	20,000
France (Somme Deposits)	,,	170,000
Do. (Other Deposits)	,,	200,000
Belgium (Mons District)	,,	150,000
Do. (Liège District)	,,	50,000
Germany	,,	30,000
Norway	,,	10,000
Canada..	,,	26,000
South Carolina (Land Deposits)	,,	300,000
Do. (River Deposits)	,,	237,000
Florida..	,,	40,000
West Indian Islands..	,,	50,000
Other Sources	,,	20,000
		1,303,000

This rapid development is most remarkable, and clearly shows a great future for the phosphate mining industry. Agriculture and the demand for phosphoric acid are indissolubly connected, and with the gradual though certain exhaustion of the earth's soil there must be an ever increasing demand for phosphoric acid to be replaced therein. It has been stated on good authority that the United States are only using one quarter of the quantity of fertilisers which should be employed to keep pace with the annual extraction of the fertilising elements from the soil. In Europe the manufacture and use of fertilisers in countries, which a few years ago were content to do without them, is making rapid strides. In fact the recognition of the importance of phosphoric acid is apparent on all sides.

It seems safe therefore to assert that the phosphate mining industry is still in its infancy, and that its future growth and development are an absolute certainty.

CLASSIFICATION OF MINERAL PHOSPHATES.

No exact geological classification of the various deposits of phosphate has yet been made owing to the great difficulty of deciding definitely to which formation certain deposits really belong, for not only does the phosphate itself assume a great variety of forms, but the sundry varieties also blend into one another in a most perplexing manner.

The ordinary classification is a non-geological one, and divides phosphates into mineral phosphates, whose origin cannot be traced to animal life, and rock phosphates (more or less mineralised) of organic origin.

The only pure mineral phosphates are the apatite deposits of Norway and Canada, and the apatites of Spain found in limited quantities at Jumilla, Zarza la Mayor and Ceclavin. All these phosphates are crystalline in form.

The deposits of Nassau (Germany), Lot-et-Garonne, Tarn-et-Garonne and Aveyron (south-west of France), Logrosan and Caceres (Spain) are usually placed under the division of mineral phosphates, and termed " phosphorite," an arbitrary name which has no practical significance. There is much dispute as to the origin of these phosphates, but most of the scientists attribute to them an organic origin.

The term " rock phosphates " covers the rest of the field, and includes in its different varieties phosphatic limestones, coprolites, nodular phosphates, concretionary, arenaceous or sheet rock phosphates and bone beds.

Having thus described the manner in which the phosphate mining industry came into existence, and given a rough outline of its development, we will now proceed to a fuller account of the phosphate deposits of Florida, South Carolina and Canada.

CHAPTER II.

—

FLORIDA PHOSPHATES.

THEIR DISCOVERY.

The existence of phosphate deposits in Florida has been known for many years, but owing to a general belief that the quantity was limited and the quality not commercially valuable, no regular examination was commenced until the close of the year 1880.

The first to discover and appreciate the true value and extent of the phosphates in South Florida was Mr. J. Francis Le Baron, of Jacksonville, who, while making a survey on behalf of the Government in the early months of the year 1881, came across the bars and beds of phosphate in Peace River. He at once recognised the fact that the numerous bones and teeth, hitherto considered merely interesting curiosities, were phosphatic, and that the deposit was one of enormous value. His work at that time prevented him from taking steps towards reaping any advantage from his discovery, and it was not until December, 1886, that he was able to

visit the locality again. He then communicated with some
northern capitalists, for whom he made a full report, dated
January, 1887, advising the purchase of about 10,000 acres.

His negotiations for acquiring the lands seem to have
been protracted and finally to have proved unsuccessful, and
his golden opportunity was lost, for Colonel G. W. Scott, of
the G W. Scott Manufacturing Company, Atlanta, Georgia,
had in the meantime heard of the deposits, and after a careful
survey, made very extensive purchases on the Peace River.

In the summer of the same year Mr. T. S. Moorehead, of
Pennsylvania, who had learnt from Mr. Le Baron that there
was phosphate in Florida, though the secret of its location
had not been mentioned to him, came south to look for the
deposit, and was fortunate enough to discover and purchase
the now famous bars at Arcadia. Supported by Colonel Scott,
who agreed to purchase all his output, Mr. Moorehead
started actual operations on a very small scale, under the
name of the Arcadia Phosphate Company, and in May, 1888,
the first shipment of Florida phosphate was made, ten car-loads
being dispatched to Colonel Scott's fertiliser works in Atlanta,
Georgia.

Shipments of phosphate were now made regularly to
Colonel Scott's works, and though the railroad cars were
actually labelled " Florida Peace River Phosphate for the G. W.
Scott Manufacturing Company," more than twelve months
elapsed before the outside world appears to have taken notice
of this new industry.

Following upon the steps of these developments in Southern Florida came the news in 1889 of the existence of phosphates in Marion County. It was in May of that year that Mr. Albertus Voght, while sinking a well near Dunnellon, noticed some rock which aroused his curiosity, and which upon analysis proved to be high-grade phosphate. This fact transpired in the autumn of that year, and led to an epidemic of prospecting, the results of which were so surprising that in a very short space of time an excitement and fever set in, which have not been parallelled since the Pacific Coast gold craze of some forty years ago. Every train was crowded with prospecting parties armed with spades and with shovels, with chemicals and with camping-out apparatus. The backwoods were dotted with numerous camps ; diggers were hired at fancy prices, and the lucky owners of vehicles and animals of any kind found their exorbitant demands readily agreed to. Men who had been trying in vain to get rid of their lands at any price suddenly found themselves independent for life ; where single dollars had been eagerly sought, fifties were now refused, and hundreds readily offered and paid. Speculators invaded every town : lands were bought up right and left regardless of prices, resold again at still higher prices, until the newspapers seriously stated that Florida was richer than the whole of the rest of the United States put together. A few head-lines from leading newspapers may be mentioned to show the state of the public pulse, "the entire gulf a rich phosphate bed" ; "millions on millions in it" ; "an acre worth from $30,000 to $12,000,000" ; "a gigantic bonanza" ; "waste lands will blossom as the rose"; "millions of money in South Florida lands"; "Marion, Citrus, and Hernando Counties to become a veritable El Dorado."

DESCRIPTION OF FLORIDA.

The popular idea that Florida was a flat country composed of alternate areas of deep sand-banks and impassable swamps seems to have prevailed even in Washington, for the Geological Survey of the U.S.A., which has done such thorough and valuable work in other States, omitted Florida entirely from the scope of their investigations. Consequently there is a great void of scientific data upon the geology of the State, and the only available information to be found is contained in the short treatises of Le Conte and Agassiz, a summary of which with additional notes appeared in an article by Professor Eugene A. Smith, published in 1881, in Vol. XXI. of the *American Journal of Science.* The unexpected discovery of phosphates has led to the commencement of a topographical survey by the Government, to be followed by a geological survey, but the work before that department is so arduous and extensive that no results or official reports can be expected for many months to come.

Speaking topographically, Florida may be described as an undulating low-lying peninsula, the highest point being

200 feet, and the average elevation about 80 feet above the level of the sea. The whole country is a succession of gently sloping ridges, connected in some places by extensive plateaux, in others by low-lying swamps. The ridges and plateaux are for the most part composed of sand and covered by a growth of pine trees, which in some places are excellent timber forests, in others merely thin saplings. The low-lying lands, which are called "hommocks," are covered with a rich soil, and where not too swampy are selected for cultivation. In the swamps every variety of tropical vegetation, more or less dense, is to be found in luxuriant abundance.

The altitudes of different places in the peninsula being of interest, the following may be mentioned. Starting from Fernandina on the north-east, and travelling in a south-westerly direction to the port of Cedar Keys, the following elevations are to be remarked: Maxwell (56 miles), 57 feet above mean low water; Trail Ridge (61 miles), 210 feet; Gainesville, 128 feet; Waldo, 150 feet; Ocala, 100 feet (with a ridge one mile below the town of 160 feet). Going south from Ocala: Pemberton Ferry, 54 feet; Lakeland, 244 feet; Plant City (west of Lakeland), 132 feet; Bartow (south-east of Lakeland), 114 feet.

Some of these altitudes are railway levels only, but the figures are sufficiently accurate to give the general impression required. Polk County has a considerable ridge running north and south, a few miles to the west of Peace River and of the Florida Southern Railroad. This ridge forms the backbone of

the south half of the peninsula, and gradually flattens out below
Bowling Green, south of which the county is almost level. It
is in this southern part that the immense grass prairies and
impassable everglades are situated.

The phosphate deposits occur on the western side of the
peninsula, and to use very wide and general terms, may be said
to be found in every county from Talahassee to Charlotte
Harbour.

In order to describe the deposits in greater detail, it is
necessary to divide the subject into two main branches, viz.,
the pebble deposits of South Florida, and the rock deposits
of Northern Florida.

THE PEBBLE DEPOSITS.

It is absolutely impossible at the present date to define
the area containing the pebble deposits, but for the purposes
of this description, the counties of Polk, Hillsborough, Manatee
and De Soto, embracing about 2,000 square miles, may be
stated to be underlaid, more or less, at varying depths, with
pebble phosphate. Polk and De Soto Counties contain the
more important deposits, and the main fields which are being
exploited at the present time are in the lands drained by the

Peace and Alafia Rivers and their numerous tributaries, and in the beds of these same rivers and streams. What appears to be the main deposit is situated on the high lands (maximum 165 feet above mean tide level), which form the watershed of the head waters of the Alafia River and of the creeks which flow into Peace River between Bartow and Bowling Green. The rough boundaries of this area would be Lakeland on the north, Bartow and Bowling Green on the east and south, and Chicora on the west. The phosphate-bearing stratum varies in thickness from a few inches to more than 30 feet, and is covered by an overburden differing in composition and thickness according to locality. Near the edges of the numerous streams, or " branches," the overburden is not heavy, but in the higher lands, dotted with shallow ponds and lakes, the phosphate is not generally reached until some 10 to 15 feet of overlying earth, sand, &c., have been removed.

The composition of the overburden is as follows :—

(i.)   Soil and subsoil : a few inches to 6 feet.

(ii.)   A light-coloured sand : a few inches to 10 feet.

(iii.)   A variously-coloured stiff clay. This clay, after the first few inches, contains phosphate pebbles, which grow more and more frequent till the regular stratum is reached.

Some deposits are covered with a rock capping of sandstone, either in the form of conglomerates or of loose rounded pieces. Occasionally it is solid rock, and crops out on the surface, and is completely honeycombed. The colour runs from rusty brown to pure white. The thickness of this sandstone capping, which is generally local in its occurrence, is rarely more than two or three feet, but it is hard to remove when conglomerated, or in rock form.

The matrix of the stratum, in which the pebbles are found, is generally argillaceous and plastic, and the proportion of sand contained therein varies in each locality. In order to ascertain the exact composition of this matrix we sent a sample, taken from the location known as Phosphoria, to Dr. Wyatt's laboratory, for complete analysis, and received the following results :—

Matrix dried at 212°.

Organic Matter	..	..	..	..	2.40
'Phosphoric Acid	..	..	..	..	15.29
†Carbonic Acid ..	..	..	..	..	6.70
Lime	..	..	..	..	20.00
Iron and Alumina	..	..	..	..	13.06
Fluoride and Magnesia	..		..	..	.60
Insoluble Silicates and Sand			..	..	41.95
					100.00

'Equivalent to Tribasic Phosphate of Lime	42.33
† „ „ Carbonate of Lime	15.20

An analysis by Dr. Maynwald of a sample taken from the Pharr deposit gave Phosphoric Acid 13.93, equivalent to Tribasic Phosphate of Lime 30.37, Iron and Alumina 9.90.

The east side of the main deposit, *i.e.*, from about two miles below Bartow, as far as Fort Meade, is quite different to the centre, for the phosphate in that region is found embedded in a hard matrix. At times it is hardly possible to distinguish between the pebbles and the matrix, both being pure white; in other places the matrix is brown in colour. The composition of this matrix does not differ from that of the phosphate pebbles it contains as much as would naturally be expected. The percentage of sand is small, and though the iron and alumina run high, there is a large percentage of phosphate of lime, so much so that at Homeland the pebble and matrix are dried and ground together, to a 100-mesh size, and sold as a fertiliser for direct application, a small quantity of the sand being blown off during the grinding. The name of the Company carrying on this business is the Whitaker Phosphate and Fertiliser Company. The analysis of the rock as taken from the ground is as follows :—

Phosphoric Acid..	29 13
Equivalent to Tribasic Phosphate of Lime..	63.50
Iron and Alumina	13.41

It appears, therefore, that the larger part of the matrix has been formed by small particles of whitish phosphate, which have acted as a binder between the pebbles.

There is yet another form of deposit, which is found about one mile south of Bartow, underlying a very small area. This appears to be a hard rock deposit, and the samples exhibited therefrom show no sign whatever of pebble formation. The analysis runs over 70 per cent. of phosphate, with about $2\frac{1}{2}$ per cent. of iron and alumina. The rock has a close resemblance to some specimens found in Marion County.

DESCRIPTION OF THE PHOSPHATE PEBBLES.

The phosphate pebbles vary in size from the tiniest specks imaginable up to potato size, the average may be said to run between one and a-half inches and one thirty-second part of an inch. They have no regular shape or appearance, sometimes their surface is smooth and polished, at other times it is much indurated and rough. The colour also varies very materially, even in the same piece of stratum. We have selected the following varieties as being representative of the different kinds of pebble :—

(i.) A pure white to cream-coloured variety, smooth and lozenge shaped, with a hard enamel surface and white interior.

(ii.) A white chalky variety, soft in composition and easily crushed by the teeth ; lozenge shaped.

(iii.) A brown variety, partially covered with a cream to blue-coloured enamel, polished surface, and very hard.

(iv.) A light brown amber-coloured, changing at times to a dark chestnut brown variety, with hard smooth and polished surface, interior is brown but lighter in shade; lozenge shaped.

(v.) A mud-coloured brown variety, with rough surface and jagged edges, very hard. These pebbles are usually found in the small creeks, and also in the upper part of the Peace River.

(vi.) A bright slatey-blue and white variety, very hard. In the larger pebbles the surface is much indurated, the smaller pieces being smooth and lozenge shaped.

(vii.) A purple-blue or plum-coloured variety. The pebbles of this colour are larger than the average size, and are to be found in Bone Valley. Their surface is hard and indurated.

(viii.) A white porous variety. These are mostly found in the neighbourhood of Little Pain's Creek, and are high in iron and alumina; lozenge shaped.

(ix.) A small hard jagged variety, with broken edges and hard surface; found everywhere; white to cream-colour.

(x.) A broken variety, light in specific gravity, and easily broken by the fingers; very porous. Found mostly north of Bartow, high in phosphate and also in iron and alumina.

All of the above varieties may be met with in any of the land pebble deposits, and seem to be intermixed generally.

(xi.) A hard jet black or blue black variety, with bright enamel surface. These are the pebbles found in all the Peace and Alafia River deposits.

(xii.) A black kidney-shaped variety: hard, but with no surface polish ; also found in Peace River.

(xiii.) A light slate-coloured variety ; much indurated. Found in the older river beds, above present water level of the Peace River.

(xiv.) A dark brown variety, very highly polished, with enamel surface : smooth and hard. These are found in the Manatee River and on its banks, and also at Sarasota.

(xv.) A light brown sandy-coloured variety : lighter in the centre than at the outside. Generally more or less rounded : surface rough. Manatee River. This variety is really a semi-phosphatised sand-tone rock.

(xvi.) A chalky-coloured variety. Found in the Caloosa-hatchie and underlying its banks. Light in specific gravity and of medium hardness. Low in analysis.

It is to be noticed that most of the pebbles, which are more than about an inch in length, are really conglomerated from smaller pebbles, even though their surface is hard and polished. The interior is composed of small hard pebbles and of a whitish powder, which has almost the same chemical analysis as the pebble, though the proportion of iron and alumina is in excess of the general average.

ANALYSIS OF THE LAND PEBBLES.

The phosphate pebbles underlying the land vary in test between 60 and 75 per cent. phosphate of lime, occasionally small samples have analysed as high as 84 per cent. The general average of land pebbles may be said to be between 65 and 70 per cent. The following is a complete analysis made by Dr. Francis Wyatt, of New York, of land pebble dried to 212°:—

Organic Matter	2.75
*Phosphoric Acid	32.19
Carbonic Acid ..	3.95
Lime	42.86
Iron and Alumina	4.20
Fluoride and Magnesia	2.25
Insoluble Siliceous	11.80
	100.00

* Equivalent to Tribasic Phosphate of Lime .. 70.21

Part of the same sample was analysed by Dr. C. Kirberger, of Hamburg, whose results gave :—

Tribasic Phosphate of Lime ..	67.12
Oxide of Iron and Alumina ..	2.88
Insoluble Siliceous Matter ..	8.50

The average results of 36 analyses made by Dr. C. Kirberger, Hamburg, of bulk samples (half-ton each), taken from various parts of the deposit at Phosphoria gave phosphate 67.35, iron and alumina 2.27 ; while the following full analyses were made in London from large average samples fairly representing the land pebble deposit of Polk County.

	A. Voelcker & Sons.	Cannon and Newton. Dried at 212°
Moisture	.45	
Organic Matter and Water of Combination	1.55	—
* Phosphoric Acid	33.07	33.26
Lime	45.82	43.86
Oxide of Iron	1.19	1.80
Alumina	1.63	
Magnesia, &c.	5.37	—
† Carbonic Acid	1.64	2.00
Insoluble Siliceous Matter	9.28	10.21
		Undetermined 8.87
	100.00	100.00
* Equal to Tribasic Phosphate of Lime	72.19	72.61
† „ Carbonate of Lime.. ..	3.72	4.54

ANALYSIS OF THE RIVER PEBBLES.

The land and river pebbles are of the same origin beyond any possible doubt, but their composition has been changed since the time when they lay in their original bed. The river pebbles analyse from 60 to 63 per cent. phosphate of lime, with an average of about 2 per cent. of iron and alumina. The following analyses may be taken as representing the average cargo :—

PEACE RIVER PHOSPHATE.

	CARGO OF 2,000 TONS.			CARGO OF 1,000 TONS.	
	Voelcker.	Dyer.	Shepard.	Dyer.	Tesche-macher.
Phosphoric Acid (dry basis) ..	28.03	27.91	28.00	28.62	28.75
equivalent to					
Tribasic Phosphate of Lime ..	61.20	60.93	61.12	62.48	62.76
Lime	40.95	41.52	41.21	42.56	43.90
Oxide of Iron	.84	1.01 } 0.80		{ 0.81 } 2.25	
Alumina	.93	1.56 }		{ 1.59 }	

The pebbles of the Alafia River have the same chemical composition, but the analysis of shipments varies in accordance with the proportion of silicates left mixed with the phosphate.

FORMATION OF THE VARIOUS PEBBLE DEPOSITS.

At the present time no definite theory has been formulated as to the exact origin of the phosphate pebbles and the formation of the deposits in which they are found; in fact, the industry is not yet sufficiently developed to afford the data upon which to argue the question on a true scientific basis.

The only known geological fact with reference to Florida is that the whole peninsula is underlaid with white limestone of Vicksburg age (lower Upper Eocene according to Sir Charles

Lyell; upper Middle Eocene according to American geologists), which is the oldest rock in Florida. It is therefore natural to suppose that Florida remained submerged until near the end of the Eocene period, after which the first elevation above the sea took place. Then came the Miocene submergence, followed by a second elevation. The next geological change would be during the Champlain period, when the land once more disappeared from sight and was covered with a mantle of sands and clays before it finally rose to its present elevation above the sea.

The phosphate pebbles had been formed before this last submergence, probably in one great deposit, and it seems not unnatural to account for the minor deposits as being composed of the washings or overflow of this main deposit, the encroaching seas having washed out from their original bed huge quantities of phosphate pebbles, mixing them with clay and sand and spreading them with tolerable evenness over the surrounding areas, with a tendency to roll them in larger quantities near or in the more depressed portions of the limestone rock.

The present rivers would subsequently cut through these layers of phosphate, washing out the sands and clays and depositing the pebble in the bottom. No doubt the rivers were wider in those days, as their channels had not yet been cut, and as time passed the channels would deepen and narrow, and the rivers would change their courses, always leaving in their older beds the pebbles they had washed from the strata now above the

ordinary level of the water. An examination of the Peace
River at Arcadia shows the smaller and smoother pebble in the
sand bars in the river's bed, while some feet above the water is
to be found an even layer of larger and rougher pebble in
the bank, covered with an overburden of sand. This feature
is also observable at many other points.

PEACE RIVER PHOSPHATE MINING.

Peace River rises near Bartow in the high lake lands of
Polk County, and flowing southward to Charlotte Harbour
empties its waters into the Gulf of Mexico. It is the fastest
flowing river in Florida, and the most irregular, and its channel
changes like that of the Mississippi. The whole river is a
constant succession of shallows and deep basins, and its
meanderings have formed the numerous bars and beds of
phosphate and sand. At many points where the bed has
become clogged up with sand and phosphate, washed from
adjoining lands and elsewhere, new channels have been made,
and the old bed remains to-day a mixture of sand and phosphate awaiting the advent of the miner.

The principal tributaries of the Peace River are Charlie
Apopka, Bowlegs, Chillocohatchee, Thompson, Pains and
Whidden Creeks, which between them drain a very large area
of country. The heavy deluges of rain which fall during the

summer months cause the small rivulet of the morning to be a
swollen stream in the evening ; the stream in like manner
becomes a torrent, and the raging, whirling, fast-flowing
streams, torrents and rivers lash and wash out the banks in
their rapid course, undermining and detaching the nodules of
phosphate from their strata and driving them ever along the
river bed.   Imagine the continuance of this process for tens of
thousands of years, and it is not difficult to find the *raison
d'être* of the drift deposits of phosphate in the Peace and other
Rivers.   In the dry season a great proportion of these bars of
phosphate with sand intermixed is above the water's surface,
and the original work was carried on by spade and wheel-
barrow, as much as 5,600 tons having been taken in this
manner from the famous bar at Arcadia.   In examining closely
this river phosphate one is surprised to find how large a
quantity there is of actual teeth, ribs, vertebræ, scales and bones,
once the component parts of beasts and birds, of fishes and
reptiles, of manatee, of elephant, of glyptodon, of mastodon, of
crocodile, and of shark.

The method of raising the phosphate at the present date
is by a 6 to 10-inch centrifugal suction pump driven by steam
power and operated upon a barge.   The suction pipe extends
from the upper deck into the water ahead of the barge, and is
adjustable by ropes and pulleys.   The phosphate is discharged
from the pipe into a revolving screen (with openings one-
sixteenth of an inch wide and a half-inch long), which shakes
and washes out a considerable quantity of the sand which falls

with the water again into the river, while the phosphate is discharged alongside through a shoot on to the scow which conveys the phosphate down the river to the works. There it is hoisted from the barge, passes through the drier, and after one more screening is ready for market.

It would probably be of service to make use of a double screen at those places on the river where the pebble is mixed with marl clay and wood drift, the centre and coarser screen separating this waste admixture and discharging it back into the river. At the present time this separation is being carried on at the works, necessitating an extra process and handling of the waste. A double screen would also be of use where no such separation is required, the coarser screen retaining the larger pebble, thus enabling the finer one to clean the smaller pebbles more efficiently than where all sizes are mixed together. This would also prevent the slots of the screens being worn out and enlarged by the constant friction of the larger pebbles. Both screens would deliver their final contents into the same shoot.

At the different works various methods of drying are in use. The favourite system seems to be the rotary iron drier. At one end of this a brick furnace is built, the phosphate is fed into the machine at the opposite end, and as the inside has flanges of iron in screw form, the phosphate is driven towards the furnace (the flames of which pass through the entire length of the drier), and drops into a feed just before reaching the fire; thence it is elevated into a screen which separates the

remaining sand from the phosphate. Another form of drier is the brick chimney with ledges inside. The phosphate is fed into the top, and as it falls from ledge to ledge the flames of the furnace evaporate the moisture. A third drier is a long, steep brick flue, down which the phosphate slides, being subjected all the time to the flames from the fires below. The objection to this method is the tendency to "avalanche;" in other words, the phosphate does not always move down the flue with regularity, but sometimes falls with a big rush, in which case the result is a mixture of red-hot and absolutely wet pebbles. It must be remembered that the pebble after washing has from 10 to 20 per cent. of moisture adhering to it.

The initial difficulties of this river-mining enterprise can only be fully understood by those who are acquainted with the natural obstacles to be confronted in an undeveloped country like Florida. The distance from which the machinery had to be brought, in most instances from Ohio, a journey of 1,200 miles, was a mere bagatelle compared to the troubles which commenced when the machinery arrived at the nearest railway station. Roads had to be cut to the river's bank, and the haulage of machinery and lumber from the railway to the location for the works often cost more and occupied as much time as the long railway transport. Next came the scarcity of any labour, with the still greater trouble of securing skilled mechanics. The initial screens, &c., had often to be thrown away and new ones designed and brought to the spot. The breakage of a small part would entail long delays, for machine-

shops are few and far between in Florida. Finally, these
initial trials and difficulties were overcome, and the pioneers
of the river phosphate mining succeeded in producing a
marketable and valuable product at less cost than phosphate
has hitherto been produced in any part of the world.

It was one thing, however, to have phosphate ready for
market at the works, and another to get it afloat at the sea-
board. The earlier companies were not situated near
navigable water, and branch spurs had to be made to the main
railroad, and the phosphate transported to Punta Gorda.
Here the trouble commenced afresh, for Punta Gorda is not a
deep seaport, and steamers can only load to 11 feet at the pier ;
the remainder of the cargo had therefore to be put into
lighters and towed a distance of 20 miles to deep water before
the loading could be completed. This necessitated the
building of lighters and steam tugs.

Some of the later companies lower down the river have
their works on water of sufficient depth to allow the phosphate
to be lightered from the works to alongside the steamers at
their loading stations in Charlotte Harbour, which reduces
their cost of shipping by about 75 cents per ton.

The dredging operations, too, are not so simple as might
be imagined, for Peace River is but a small stream during eight
months of the year, and the barges often get stuck in the
shallow places, and have to pump out the sand before they can
move from place to place. It seems a strange oversight

that the barges are not fitted with steam winches which could pull them through the lighter sand-banks, whereas now hand-labour has to be depended upon, causing frequent delays. In the summer months the river is about 17 feet higher than during the winter, and the stream is so deep and rapid that pumping has from time to time to be absolutely suspended. The river's banks are overflowed, and the water invades even the actual works. The drifts or bars of phosphate vary much in their composition : sometimes there is but little phosphate ; at others, as much as 60 or 70 per cent. of the mass. At Liverpool and Cleveland, where the tide is felt, there seems to be an immeasurably large quantity of phosphate, for the incoming tides have prevented the pebbles from being rolled further than this point. On the other hand, the same causes have retained mud and clay, which constitute a drawback and prevent the mining operations being carried on here as easily as elsewhere.

Going up stream it is apparent that the rock bed of the river has depressions or basins of extended area. It is here that the bars have been formed, and enormous quantities of pebble have been taken from very small areas, the thickness of phosphate-bearing bars or drifts being in some places as much as 17 feet. Sometimes, after one of these drifts has been exhausted, a second trial has yielded as much pebble as the first, the freshets having in the meantime refilled the exhausted basin with sand and phosphate. In some places there is an absence of sand and phosphate for miles and miles, where

the river's bed is composed of smooth rock. Just above
Zolfo there is one mile and a-half of rock bottom, then a
basin of sand and phosphate extending about half a-mile;
then rock bottom for another mile leading to a large basin
at Wauchula, about three-quarters of a-mile in length.
Occasionally the sand has formed a stratum of hard-pan,
below which further drifts of phosphate and sand are frequently
discovered.

There seems to be an impression prevailing pretty widely
in Florida, that the drift deposits in the river will be exhausted
in a few years. This, however, is not likely to prove correct,
at all events near the mouth of the river, for the Peace River
has, in the lapse of bygone ages, covered an area varying from
half a-mile to two miles in its meandering changes. The
present bed of the river is but a trifle compared to this, so that
even supposing the bottom of to-day's river bed to be exhausted,
there is still many times the same quantity left in the adjoining
sand-banks, once the bed of the river. The natural way to
work these drifts would be to divert the river's course by
building dams in the dry season, and cause the river
to wash out the sand from its older beds. Between Fort Meade
and Big Pain's Creek the old river bed has not only become
filled up with sand, but in many cases is indistinguishable
from the mainland, until pits are sunk which reveal the work
of earlier ages and show the drifts of washed river pebble
beneath the present level surface of sand and earth. Sometimes these drifts are found super-imposed upon the even layers

of phosphate deposit with clay matrix. Some of the newer companies working north of Bowling Green, whose river area is limited, intend working the adjoining land deposits when they have exhausted the present and old river beds, and will then employ steam excavators for removing the overburden. The river drifts in this neighbourhood are rarely more than seven feet in thickness, and a tolerably accurate estimate can be made of the contents of a given area of river deposit.

An erroneous idea is sometimes cited that the rivers are redepositing pebbles as fast as they are being extracted. This idea has apparently come from the fact that freshets occasionally uncover drifts which had been unnoticed before, and also that the drifts break up from time to time only to form afresh lower down the river, for it is quite certain that the quantity of new pebble actually washed into the river's bed is infinitesimally small. It is most interesting to notice the change in the colour of the pebbles, which are found to be a lightish brown colour near Bartow, a darker brown south of Fort Meade, and an absolute blue-black at Zolfo and further south. There are, of course, black pebbles all along the river's bed, but the above changes are worth noticing.

South of Zolfo the pebble is fairly free from impurities, but the further north that examinations are made will be found increasing quantities of wood drift, clay balls, and carbonate rock mixed up with pebbles.

NAMES OF COMPANIES IN OPERATION ON PEACE RIVER.

At the close of 1890, the following Companies were in operation :—

Name.	Works at.	Capital.	Acres Owned.
Arcadia Phosphate Co.	Arcadia	$300,000	1,000
De Soto Phosphate Mining Co.	Zolfo	250,000	4,100
Peace River Phosphate Co.	Arcadia	300,000	9,800

With a daily output of about 200 tons.

Since that date the following Companies have commenced operations* :—

Name.	Works at.	Capital.	Acres Owned.
Jacksonville Peace River Phosphate Co.	Apopka	$1,000,000	1,480
Charlotte Harbour Phosphate Co.	Fort Ogden	350,000	7,500
Gulf Phosphate Mining and Manufacturing Co.	Cleveland	240,000	5,200
South Florida Phosphate Co.	Liverpool	480,000	1,500
National Peace River Co.	Langford's Bridge	100,000	700
United States Phosphate Co.	,, ,,	———	680

The average daily yield of an 8-inch pump is from thirty-five to forty-five tons of pebble, though from time to

*Note.—There are some smaller companies in addition to these, but as far as we could ascertain, no regular output has been made, nor will the quantities be likely to affect the market. There are also other Companies organised, but not at work.

time when an exceptionally fine drift has been found, one pump has produced as much as seventy-five tons. There are at present twelve pumps in operation and three more will be added very shortly, so that when all the plants are working, the extreme limit to the weekly capacity is 4,000 tons. Allowing for the usual contingencies a total quantity of 100,000 to 125,000 tons for 1892 is not likely to be exceeded.

A great many wild reports have been circulated and even printed about the colossal output to be made months and months ago by the Peace River Companies. As a matter of fact their present output is a marvel, considering the huge difficulties which have been successfully contended with, and the record of shipments made speaks a volume of praise on behalf of the pluck, perseverance and energy of those who have used their brains, time and money in producing these results.

It is an easy matter to speak glibly of a daily output of 100 tons, but it takes a long time to arrive at this figure, and many alterations both small and great have generally to be effected in the machinery before any regular daily output, however small, can be made. Much experience has now been gained, and the new comers are able to profit thereby. The output of the various companies can of course be increased by putting in extra plant, but this is likely to be done in proportion only to the growth of the demand for the pebble.

ALAFIA RIVER PHOSPHATE MINING.

The Alafia River and its tributaries contain similar deposits to those in the Peace River. This river rises in Polk County, a few miles west of Bartow, and flows westward into Hillsborough Bay at a point about eight miles south of Tampa. There are at present three companies, *i.e.*, The Peruvian Phosphate Co., The Tampa Phosphate Co. and The Alafia River Phosphate Co. at work dredging in the river near Peru, a distance of about five miles from the mouth of the river. The total monthly output varies from two to three thousand tons. One company has its works on the river bank near Peru, the other two companies have built their works at Tampa.

Just above Peru the banks of the river are steep, and there is no phosphate for a distance of four miles, the bottom of the river being hard rock with scarcely any sand. Above this point the beds of phosphate occur again, but the river is very shallow and most of the pebble is mixed with clay. Two companies are going to operate near or in Turkey Creek, and will cut into the deposits underlying the banks of this stream with dipper dredges.

It is said that the whole of the actual river deposit will be exhausted in about five years' time, as the river is a small one, and its bed near the mouth has not varied much. The phosphate is identical with that of Peace River, but there appears to be more silica and small loose limestone rock in the Alafia River.

MANATEE, MYAKKA AND CALOO-SAHATCHIE RIVERS.

The Manatee River has a parallel course with the Alafia River, about 24 miles further south, and its tributaries have bars of pebble. Gamble Creek is very rich in phosphate, but the percentage of iron and alumina is said to run as high as 18 per cent., making the phosphate worthless. No mining is going on in this river, which may be said to be practically unexplored. There is an immense phosphate bed at the river's mouth, and its shores are strewn with phosphate and sandstone, amongst which there is a large proportion of bone. The phosphate is mostly black in colour, though some of the nodules are brown.

The Myakka River rises about eight miles south of the head waters of the Manatee, and flowing southwards empties its waters into Charlotte Harbour. There is plenty of phosphate all along its bed, but there is so great an admixture of silicate pebbles and shell that no mining has hitherto been attempted.

The Caloosahatchie River rises a few miles west of Lake Okechobee, and flows westward into San Carlos Bay. Mining operations were conducted in Twelve-Mile Creek, but the admixture of shell with the phosphate proved too great a difficulty, and work has been suspended in the meantime.

BLACK RIVER PHOSPHATE.

In addition to the deposits of phosphate found in the rivers of South Florida, there is also a deposit in Black Creek, a

tributary of the St. John's River. The pebble is rougher and
more jagged than the phosphate of Peace River, and there is
a greater admixture of silicate pebbles. The analysis runs from
48 to 53 per cent. of phosphate. There is one Company only,
the Black River Phosphate Company, operating this deposit,
and present daily output is said to be about 60 tons. The
bulk of this material will be used in the United States, as the
grade is too low to make European prices remunerative.

SHIPMENTS OF RIVER PHOSPHATE.

Year.	River.	By Rail. Tons.	By Water to United States. Tons.	Foreign. Tons.	Total. Tons.
1888	Peace River	.. 911	.. —	.. —	.. 911
1889	,,	.. 4,206	.. —	.. —	.. 4,206
1890	,,	.. 15,246	.. 8,130	.. 5,750	.. 29,126
,,	Black Creek	.. —	.. 2,000*	.. 850	.. 2,850
,,	Alafia River	.. 2,000*	.. —	.. —	.. 2,000
1891	Peace River	.. 18,000	.. 14,500	.. 37,000	.. 69,500
,,	Alafia River	.. —	.. —	.. —	.. *8,000
,,	Black Creek	.. 3,000*	.. 1,200	.. ...	.. 4,200

* Estimates only.

PRICE OF RIVER LANDS.

The early purchases of river lands, before the existence of
the phosphate was known, were made at prices varying from a
dollar and a-quarter to five dollars per acre. Even as late as
the autumn of 1889 large areas changed hands at prices under
$20 per acre. In the spring of 1891 many small tracts were
secured at prices varying from $20 to $50 per acre. Well

selected sections have fetched as much as $300 per acre, and at the present time when only a few small and isolated patches remain at disposal, $100 to $200 per acre according to location is being asked. There seems to have been less speculation and excitement over the river deposits than over the land pebble deposits, as is shown by the smaller number of companies formed for mining the rivers.

The total purchases of lands made by the River Companies at present in operation have amounted to close upon one million dollars in cash, and the purchase of plant, &c., has cost a little over half a-million dollars, making a total cash investment in the river mining of about $1,500,000. To-day's value, however, would be represented by very different figures, since most of the lands were bought before their real value was appreciated.

———

DUTY ON RIVER PHOSPHATE MINING.

The following is a copy of the Florida Phosphate Law, enacted by the last Legislature and now in effect, under which the State of Florida collects a royalty on all phosphates taken from her navigable waters :—

" *Be it Enacted by the Legislature of the State of Florida:*

" SECTION I. That the Governor, Comptroller and the Attorney-General of the State of Florida be, and they are hereby constituted a Board of Phosphate Commissioners;

which Board shall have the control and management of the
phosphate interests of the State of Florida, in the beds of her
navigable waters and of all the phosphate rock and phosphatic deposits therein, and which may be dug, mined and
removed therefrom to the extent of the State's interests
therein. The said Board is authorised for and in behalf of
the State of Florida, to enter into contracts with all persons
desiring to avail themselves of the provisions of this Act in
conformity therewith, and to take such means as may be
necessary to collect all such sum or sums, which are or may
become due to the State of Florida on account of the phosphate rock and phosphatic deposits dug, mined or removed
from the beds of such navigable waters of the State.

"Sec. 2. The State of Florida hereby grants the right to
persons, natural or corporate, to dig, mine and remove from the
beds of navigable waters of the State, any and all phosphate rock
and phosphatic deposits therein, upon the terms and conditions
as follows, to wit: That there shall be paid to the State of
Florida the sum of fifty cents per ton for every ton of phosphate rock or phosphatic deposit analysing fifty per cent. or
less, and not exceeding fifty-five per cent. bone phosphate of
lime, so mined, dug and removed; seventy-five cents per ton
for every ton of phosphate rock or phosphatic deposit analysing
over fifty-five per cent. and not exceeding sixty per cent.
phosphate of lime, so mined, dug or removed; one dollar per
ton on every ton of phosphate rock or phosphatic deposit
analysing in excess of sixty per cent. bone phosphate of lime,

so mined, dug and removed, an account of which shall be rendered quarterly to the Board of Phosphate Commissioners, and payment shall be made quarterly to the Treasurer of the State of Florida for all phosphate rock and phosphatic deposits so mined, dug and removed during the quarter. *Provided,* That no person or persons shall be permitted to dig, mine or remove any phosphate rock or phosphatic deposit from the bed of any navigable waters of the State of Florida, until he or they shall have first entered into a contract with the Board of Phosphate Commissioners, in conformity with the provisions of this Act, and shall file with such Board a bond with good and sufficient sureties, either personal or by a guaranty company to be approved by the Board, in such sum as the Board shall deem proper; conditions to comply with the terms of such contract and the provisions of this Act.

" Sec. 3.   The Board of Phosphate Commissioners are authorised to give or contract for the exclusive right to dig, mine and remove phosphate rock or phosphatic deposits from the beds of the navigable waters of the State within certain well defined limits and for a period not to exceed five years. In granting such rights, the Board of Phosphate Commissioners shall require that the person or persons, company or companies shall begin mining within six months from the date of the contract, and that such mining shall be continued the full term of the contract, unless the phosphate or phosphatic deposit be exhausted.   The Board shall give preference to riparian owners, also to those who may have commenced mining or preparing to mine prior to the passage of this Act but riparian owners and persons having commenced mining or preparing, in good faith, to mine and remove such phosphates shall make application for a contract and file his or their bond, as herein provided, within sixty days from the date of notice that any application has been made in good faith by others for such contract, which notice shall be given by the Board of Phosphate Commissioners. *Provided*, That such contracts shall in no case exceed ten miles by the course of said stream. *Provided also,* That the provisions of this Act shall not be construed as applying in cases of navigable streams or any part thereof that is not meandered, and the ownership of the lands embracing which is vested in a legal purchaser.

"SEC. 4. That the Board of Phosphate Commissioners are authorised to appoint an Inspector of Phosphate at a salary not to exceed $1,500 per annum, whose duty it shall be under the direction of said Board, to visit and inspect the works and operations of all persons mining or removing phosphate rock or phosphatic deposits from the bed of navigable waters of the State, to analyse or cause to be analysed, when deemed necessary or required by the Board of Phosphate Commissioners, said phosphate rock or phosphatic deposits so mined, dug or removed, and to inspect the books and accounts of persons so mining, in the interests of the State and the furtherance of the collection of the moneys due or which shall become due to the State on account of phosphates mined, as aforesaid ; that such Inspector of Phosphates shall in all respects be and act as the executive officer of the said Board of Phosphate Commissioners.

"SEC. 5. That any person or persons who shall dig, mine or remove any phosphate rock or phosphatic deposit from the bed of any of the navigable waters of this State without complying with the terms of this Act, shall be guilty of a misdemeanour, and upon conviction thereof shall be punished by a fine not to exceed $1,000 or imprisonment in the county jail not to exceed twelve months, or by both fine and imprisonment. *Provided, however,* That the provisions of this section shall not apply to persons mining under a *bonâ fide* claim of ownership of said phosphate deposits.

"SEC. 6. That the Board of Phosphate Commissioners are authorised to institute all suits and legal proceedings in the name of the State which may be necessary to protect the rights and interests of the State, and to enforce the collections of all moneys due, or which may become due to the State on account of phosphate rock or phosphatic deposits dug, mined or removed from the bed of her navigable waters ; and for such purpose they are authorised to employ counsel at such reasonable compensation as, in their opinion, is right and proper, which, together with the salary of the Inspector of Phosphates, and all other costs and expenses which are incurred in carrying out the provisions of this Act, and in collecting the moneys due or to become due to the State for all phosphate rock and phosphatic deposits mined or removed from the bed of navigable waters of the State, including attorney's fees and other costs of suits now pending for that purpose, shall be paid out of the funds which shall be realised from the royalty paid to the State for the phosphate rock or phosphatic deposits so mined and removed.

"SEC. 7. All laws in conflict with the provisions of this Act be, and the same are hereby repealed.

"SEC. 8. This Act shall go into effect upon its approval by the Governor."

The State has made a claim on the above lines upon all the companies who have mined river pebble. Some of the companies have paid the royalty claimed, others have refused to do so. In the cases where companies or individuals have refused to pay the royalty, the State demands the whole value of the phosphate extracted, claiming ownership not only of the actual part of the bed covered by the water, but the whole width of the river's basin. The term navigable is held to apply to water down which planks could be floated, or which could be in any way used for the conveyance of the produce of the surrounding country.

It seems problematical that the State, which has itself sold lands by the acre without deducting the area covered by the river, can thus re-claim what it has itself sold. Further than this, many companies have been obliged to clean up the bed of the river even where the water is deep, by taking out the fallen trees, sunken logs, &c., which would have rendered the floating of even a plank for any continuous distance an absolute impossibility.

Should the State ultimately be successful in making good its present claims, Peace River phosphate will be subjected to a royalty of $1.00 per ton, since it is sold on a guaranteed minimum of 60 per cent.

COST OF MINING RIVER PEBBLE AND COMPARISON OF THE PHOSPHATE INDUSTRIES OF THE FLORIDA RIVERS AND THE SOUTH CAROLINA RIVERS.

In the part of this work which refers to river mining in South Carolina, it will be found that the total cost there, f.o.b. steamer, is estimated at $4.00 per ton.

The cost of preparing Florida river phosphate has been given at figures varying from 75 cents to $2.25 per ton. One of the pioneers states that his total cost to date has not exceeded $1.40 per ton, exclusive of depreciation of plant. The general cost of production f.o.b. cars at works, may be taken as about $1.75 including depreciation and wear and tear of plant. To this has to be added the royalty of $1 per ton, and about 75 cents for lighterage, where the works and operations are on navigable water, making a total of $3.50 f.o.b. Punta Gorda. Taking those works not on navigable water, and supposing the State to be unable to enforce the royalty claimed, we have the following figures, *i.e.*, estimated cost, f.o.b. cars, $1.75 per ton, railroad freight to Punta Gorda 70 cents, and lighterage, &c., 75 cents, making $3.20 per ton, or $4.20 if the royalty has to be paid. If shipments are made via Port Tampa, railroad freight and loading cost about $1.40 per ton, so that cost f.o.b. Port Tampa is the same as f.o.b. Punta Gorda.

Freights from South Carolina being cheaper by about 50 cents to 75 cents per ton than from Punta Gorda, it will be seen that there is no advantage to be gained by competition between the two industries, and it is to be hoped that when the production from Peace River becomes larger, steps will be taken to regulate the output in conjunction with the output of South Carolina, and thus avoid a senseless competition, which can do no good but very materially injure both industries.

———

LAND PEBBLE MINING.

Leaving now the subject of the river phosphate, which has been and is still to-day being washed out of the lands (though in imperceptible quantities) into the beds of the creeks and rivers, let us examine the method of working the land deposits, whence these supplies have been taken. Innumerable borings have been made, and pits sunk in all quarters, with a surprising similarity of results as regards test of the phosphate and yield of pebble to the mass. An average cubic yard of good stratum weighs about 3,600 lbs. in its natural state (which includes about 20 to 25 per cent. of moisture), and may be safely estimated to yield from 600 to 1,200 lbs. of dry pebble. Sometimes the result will be as high as 2,200 lbs., but this is exceptional, and an average of about 900 lbs. to the cubic yard (or 25 per cent. of pebble to the mass) will be about the general yield of a good deposit. This would be equivalent to 300 lbs. per square yard one foot thick, or say 600 to 650 tons per acre for each foot of phosphate deposit.

It is absolutely impossible at the present date to state the maximum thickness of the deposit, though mention may be made of the fact that it has been proved by one company to be 25 feet thick where they are operating.

The colour of the matrix varies from pure white to all shades of red, yellow, blue and green; sometimes these various colours are encountered in succession. Occasionally layers of sand or clay, from an inch to several feet in depth, are found in the phosphate stratum. The upper part of the stratum has generally more clay in the matrix, and as greater depth is reached the proportion of sand increases. The size of the pebbles is always varying: in one place at a depth of 10 feet the pebbles became very small, and it looked as if the deposit was giving out; a few feet lower the pebbles increased in size and in quantity. Thus it will be seen that no law can be laid down for their occurrence.

Testing by auger and by wells is liable to be most misleading, and pitting is therefore the only accurate method of determining the contents of a given area. In certain places where borings have been made the limestone rock has been encountered at depths varying from 25 to 35 feet, in others pebble was pumped all the way from the surface to a depth of 53 feet. In sinking artesian wells pebbles are said to have been

pumped at 250 feet from the surface ; the layer does not seem
to have been continuous, and the pebbles may possibly have
been washed in from above.

The methods of raising and preparing the phosphate seem
to be as numerous as the companies. One of the most efficient
and cheapest methods is in operation at Phosphoria (owned by
the Florida Phosphate Company, Limited, of London, England),
where a dipper dredge is being used. The employment of this
machine for the purpose in question was most severely criticised,
and failure was generally predicted, as the deposit to be
operated is situated on high lands away from any stream, and
when the barges were being built there was no water near at
hand. A pit was dug to the depth of a few feet, and the water
brought by ditches from ponds in the neighbourhood, and when
sufficient supply had come in, the barges were launched.
Contrary to the general prophecy, the water did not fall upon
the dredge beginning to work, and it seems that the water
springs about as fast as the deposit is taken out. The second
barge, containing the washing and drying machinery, is placed
alongside the one carrying the dredge machinery. The dipper
bucket drops the phosphate into a hopper (into which a stream
of water plays), at the bottom of which there are two iron rolls—
with steel teeth—running at different speeds. Below the rolls
are two long iron troughs with revolving shafts carrying
teeth fixed in screw-form, which separate the phosphate from
the matrix and carry it along. The water is fed from above, all
along the length of the washers, and escapes through sluices,

cut in the sides, a few inches above the top of the teeth, taking with it the matrix now dissolved in the water. The pump supplying the water throws 10,000 gallons per minute. At the further end of the washers perforated elevator buckets convey the phosphate into steam-jacketed driers, through which a hot air blast is driven by fan from the boiler's furnace to increase the capacity of the drier. After being dried the phosphate passes through a rotary screen which takes out the remaining sand and dust, and the phosphate is conveyed automatically on to a scow, which is floated to the storage house, where the pebble is discharged by elevators into the bins. In case absolutely clean water may be required, the Company is sinking an artesian well; it has also in contemplation the building of a brick drier on the land, should the capacity of the jacketed drier prove insufficient to keep pace with the dredge, which has a capacity of 800 to 1,000 cubic yards per day. The dredge commenced operations in November, and the washing machinery began to run in February.

The first shipment of land pebble was made by the Pharr Phosphate Company, in May, 1891. This Company owns about 700 acres of land two miles south of Bartow, and their works are situated alongside the track of the Florida Southern Railroad, and on the bank of Six-Mile Creek. The deposit is identical in character to that at Phosphoria, where Six-Mile Creek rises, and underlies the whole of the Company's property. It is covered with a sand-rock capping which is from a few inches to two feet in thickness. The digging is carried on by hand, and a small locomotive draws the loaded cars to the works, where the phosphate is discharged into a washer similar in design to the one just described. From the washer the phosphate passes into a rotary sieve with a serpent flange inside. Fresh water is fed from a pipe running through the centre of the sieve. On discharge from the screen the phosphate is dried in a steam-jacketed drier and elevated into a storage room, ready for shipment. The total production up to December, 1891, was under 1,000 tons, the numerous breakdowns and alterations incidental to an entirely new industry having caused frequent long delays.

At the works of the Bartow Phosphate Company, about one mile north of Bartow, the deposit is rather different to the general character of the neighbourhood, the phosphate being apparently broken pieces, light in specific gravity, very porous and brittle. The phosphate is being raised by a land excavator of the orange peel type, fitted with four lips and capable of excavating about 200 cubic yards in 10 hours. The washer at these works is made in three separate sections inclining upwards, through each of which the pebbles are forced upwards in succession, the water being discharged at the lower ends. The pebble is dried in the ordinary rotary iron drier. These works commenced running last October, and about 200 tons were dispatched to northern points by railroad before the end of the year.

A few miles further north is Lake Hancock, where the Peace River rises, which is underlaid with a bed of phosphate about 8 to 12 feet thick; the matrix is clay, and over the phosphate are several feet of black sedimentary mud. The Mastodon Company has been organised to mine this deposit, and has a charter from the State under which it has to pay the same royalty as the River Companies. A dipper dredge will be employed. The pebble here runs a little over 70 per cent., with between $1\frac{1}{2}$ and $2\frac{1}{2}$ per cent. of iron and alumina. This Company expects to be in operation by the spring of this year.

About nine miles west of Bartow are situated the lands of the Bone Valley Phosphate Company, through which runs a small creek, a tributary of the north fork of the Alafia River. This creek has meandered to an extent which is surprising, and though the channel is only about three feet wide, the whole bed is about 100 yards across. This area is underlaid with largish pebbles mixed in sand, constituting in reality a drift deposit, and will be mined by a centrifugal pump from a barge, the stream being dammed up to hold the water. The deposits underlying the land will be excavated by a dredge at a future date, when the bed of the creek has been exhausted.

Two miles north of Fort Meade, on Hendry Branch, the Virginia-Florida Phosphate Company owns about 300 acres of land, which slopes sharply on both sides down to the stream. The present digging, which is done by hand, is being carried on near the bed of the creek, where there is a bed of drift phosphate in sand about three feet thick. The works are situated on the

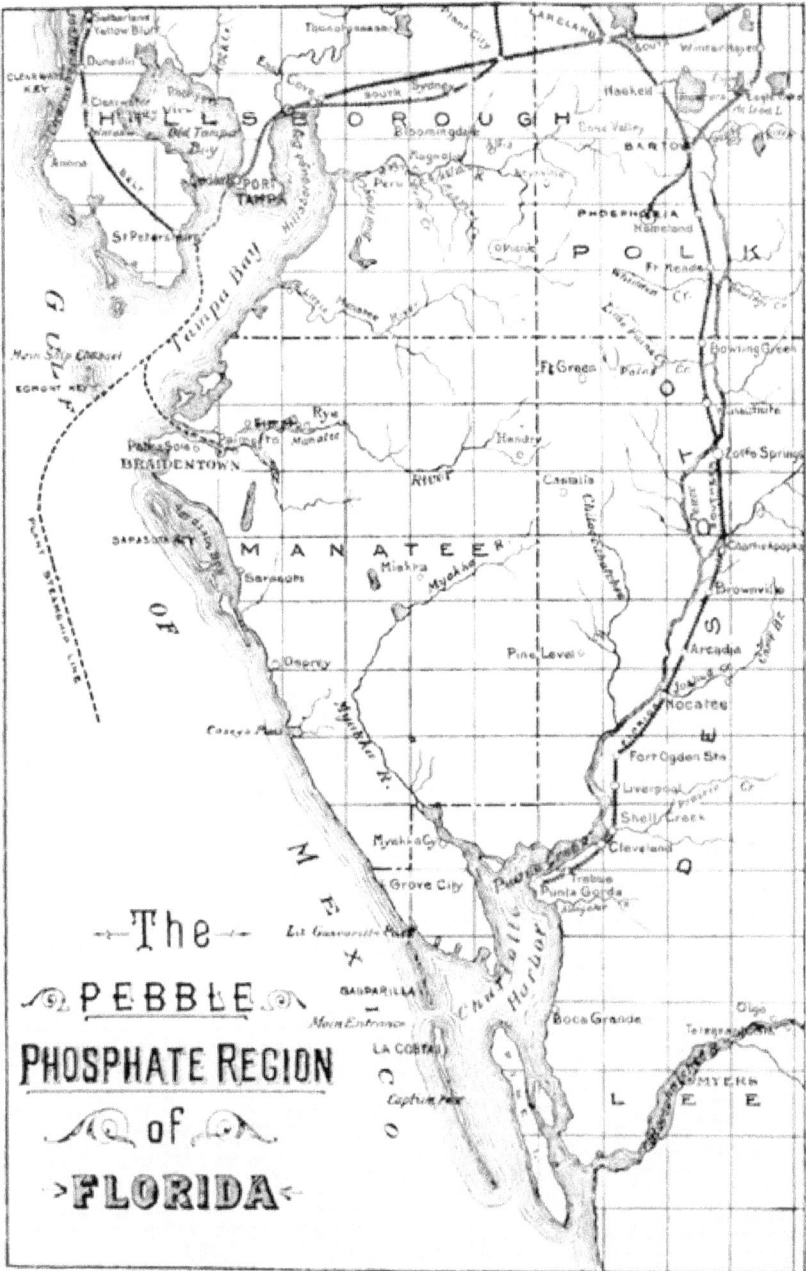

The

PEBBLE

PHOSPHATE REGION

of

FLORIDA

high ground, where the main deposit, which is said to be very thick, is overlaid by a few feet of cap rock. The water for washing is pumped from a well sunk to a depth of about 250 feet The drying is done by a brick chimney. It is under contemplation to mine by dredge or land excavator. About 1,500 tons were shipped last year, the result of some 100 days' work, extensive alterations in the plant having consumed much time.

At Fort Meade a company is mining pebble embedded in a hard white rock, which is broken up by crusher. The pebbles are then screened from the sand and matrix. Iron and alumina runs between 6 and 7 per cent.

Several other undertakings have been organised, and are getting in their plant, but the work is not forward enough to enable any description to be made.

There is a very fine deposit of pebble on Little Pain's Creek, overlaid with a white rock capping well mixed with pebbles, but no operations have been started in this neighbourhood. Big Pain's Creek also contains large deposits in its bed and under the surrounding banks, but the iron and alumina is said to run high.

It is not known at the present date how far north and east the pebble deposit extends. Lake Hancock is the present northern boundary, and the Peace River is practically the eastern boundary. Bowlegs Creek, just south of Fort Meade and east of Peace River, flows through a fine deposit, with a very stiff clay matrix; and C. Apopka River, further south, is a

museum for the palæontologist. Kissimmee Island is said to
have a deposit of black pebble, but no thorough examination
has been made of this district. At Tampa, when boring wells
for water, a phosphate stratum was found at six feet from
the surface, 12 to 16 feet in thickness. Below this a
sandstone rock, 12 feet thick, was encountered; then a
stratum of about 16 to 20 feet of clay; and then three feet
of flint, under which was the limestone rock. The Bays of
Hillsborough and Tampa are said to be underlaid with black
pebble, but the superincumbent sand is too thick for operations
to be undertaken.

The islands near the mouth of Manatee River are underlaid with a stratum of brown phosphate about one foot
thick, but the average test is low, many of the nodules
being partially phosphatised sandstone. The shores of these
islands are covered with fossil bones, which test about
74 per cent. in phosphates and 1 per cent. in iron and
alumina, but the sand rock is again present. The marl crops
out along this neighbourhood, and pieces are intermixed
with the phosphate.

Travelling south, the Sarasota region is encountered.
The phosphate deposit occurs a few feet from the surface, the
pebbles being embedded in clay. Pebble is also found in
abundance in all the small creeks. There appears to be a great
deal of semi-phosphatised sand rock in all this part of the
country, and though undoubtedly there are good deposits, yet
the average stratum in this neighbourhood is unfit for mining

purposes. In some places a quantity of small bright amber-coloured smooth pebbles are found, which run high in analysis, but the silicate pebbles which are mixed throughout more than counteract this advantage. The shores of Sarasota Bay are literally strewn with bones, mostly the ribs of the manatee, and also with the sand rock. Should a deposit be found without sand rock or silicate pebbles, mining and shipping can be carried on very cheaply. It needs a careful and long investigation to determine what tracts are suitable for mining, and while any cheap and rich phosphate deposits remain unsold in Polk County, that section is likely to have the preference.

Major E. Willis, of Charleston, South Carolina, gives the following analyses, made by Dr. C. U. Shepard, Jun., of samples taken by him when making an examination of the Sarasota tract for the proprietors :—

	Mois- ture.	Phos. Acid.	Trib. Phos.of Lime.	Do. Dry Basis.	Oxide of Iron and Almna.	Silic. Insol.	Condition of Material.
Land Rock : Large size from Bay ..	1.10	25.97	56.72	57.35	2.50	18.60	Full of Sand.
Phillipi Creek: Small Rock and Gravel..	1.05	24.05	52.53	53.09	1.63	21.60	Full of Sand.
Phillipi Creek; Free of Gravel	.95	29.04	—	64.03	3.25	8.60	Free from Sand.
North Creek: Rock) Shell Gravel ..)	1.10	21.62	47.22	47.75	1.50	16.16	{ Full of Sand { and Shell.
Land Rock: Small Rock and Gravel..	.90	26.35	57.56	58.08	2.13	17.03	Full of Sand
Land Rock: Free of Sand	.70	29.19	—	64.15	3.87	8.53	Free of Gravel.
Bone from Bowlees Creek	2.80	33.26	72.64	74.73	.50	.13	Just as Mined.

C 2

AREA AVAILABLE FOR SUCCESSFUL

LAND PEBBLE MINING.

Although such an enormous area of country is underlaid
by the phosphate deposit, it must not be thought that it is
all suitable for mining operations. As a matter of fact, the
further that practical investigations are pursued, so much
smaller do those tracts appear which are suitable for economic
working. Too great a thickness of overburden, and too thin
a phosphate stratum, immediately eliminate about 1,500 square
miles of the phosphate area. Then comes the important
question of iron and alumina which is found to be excessive
in many tracts otherwise suitable for exploitation. Heavy
sandstone capping cuts out a large acreage ; want of water
interferes in other places.

To sum up, we find that the total area likely to be mined
is probably less in extent than the Charleston phosphate fields,
though, on the other hand, those deposits which are available
in Florida are capable of producing twenty to forty times
more phosphate per acre than is raised in the South Carolina
phosphate region. The Carolina fields are within measurable
exhaustion, from an economic mining point of view, whereas
the examinations already made in Florida show an
inexhaustible mine of wealth for generations whose forefathers
are still unborn.

COST OF PRODUCTION OF LAND PEBBLE PHOSPHATE.

The cost of raising and preparing land pebble for market varies very considerably in accordance with the methods employed. The industry is too young at the present date for any actual figures to be given. Where no hand labour is employed the total cost delivered on board cars at works should not exceed $1.50 to $2.00 per ton. Freight to Port Tampa varies from $1.00 to $1.50 according to location of mines, and includes delivery to steamer alongside the pier. Thus the estimated cost f.o.b. steamer at Port Tampa would be about $2.50 to $3.50 per ton, where the best appliances are in use. Where the deposit is being worked by hand, cost will be at least $1.00 per ton higher.

LIST OF LAND PEBBLE COMPANIES

ACTUALLY IN OPERATION* OR EXPECTING TO COMMENCE VERY SHORTLY.

Name.	Address.	Capital.	Acres Owned.
Alafia Mineral Lands Co.	Plant City	—	—
*Bartow Phosphate Co.	Bartow	$250,000	—
Bone Valley Phosphate Co.	Lakeland	—	400
*Florida Phosphate Co., Ltd.	Phosphoria	1,000,000	9,000
*Fort Meade Phosphate Co.	Fort Meade	50,000	40
Land Pebble Co.		—	—
Mastodon Phosphate Co.	Bartow	—	—
*Pharr Phosphate Co.	,,	500,000	700
Terraceia Phosphate Co.	,,	1,000,000	5,600
*Virginia-Florida Phosphate Co.	Wilmott	120,000	300

It is not possible to name all of the numerous companies
which have been formed for the purpose of mining land pebble,
but the above appear to be the most important at the present
time. Several companies which have been organised are waiting
till practical results are obtained by the above companies, so that
they may be able to decide which is the best method of
operating.

THE FUTURE OF THE PEBBLE MINING INDUSTRY.

It is as yet rather premature to predict the future of the
land pebble industry, but it may not be out of place to mention
one or two points which seem to foreshadow an important
position for the land pebble mining among the various
phosphate industries of the world.

There has as yet been no discovery made of any phosphate deposit of such gigantic dimensions as to area. The
regularity of the deposit is unparalleled, and the thickness of the
stratum, taking 10 feet only as the average, is beyond anything
hitherto known to exist elsewhere.   There are in France a few
cases where the Somme phosphate has been found 30 feet in
thickness, and one instance where 40,000 tons have been taken
from 2½ acres; but the whole area of the Somme phosphate
deposits owned by the companies in operation does not exceed
1,000 acres. Who then can state the limit of the capacity of
pebble lands, when it is known that the stratum has been dug
into for 25 feet without going through it, such a stratum being able

to produce 16,000 tons per acre? In Charleston 15 inches is the average stratum, with 6 to 10 feet of overburden; in Florida the average stratum is thicker than the average overburden, and the test of the phosphate in Florida is ten units higher than that near Charleston. The test of the phosphate and the yield of pebble per cubic yard being practically invariable to any appreciable extent, this industry is based on known conditions which do not change from day to day as in other kinds of mining.

Taking these points into consideration, and with the history of Charleston mining as a guiding line, it is not wide of the mark to predict that an industry which can produce a medium testing phosphate at a figure never yet touched by other producers of the same quality, will soon take a high and important place. The increasing demand for phosphates of medium grade, together with an extending market for all phosphates, leaves no room for doubting the probable rapid growth of land pebble mining.

That there will be great competition among the companies, and the likelihood of extremely low prices for some time, is only to be expected, but in view of the expensive plant required it is probable that producers of land pebble will combine in some way rather than enter a war of competition. The necessity for heavy initial outlay will tend to keep the field from being overcrowded, and the similarity of interest should help to establish a more reasonable method of marketing the phosphate than has been the case in other phosphate centres.

River pebble had a very easy introduction into the phosphate market, for the supplies came forward at a time when such a material was actually required. The difficulties of the Coosaw Mining Company in South Carolina, and the consequent falling off of available supplies from that district, enabled large quantities to be consumed last year without weakening prices. Since river pebble is almost identical with, if not superior to South Carolina river rock, it will always be one of the phosphates most in demand.

THE ROCK DEPOSITS.

The extensive prospecting that followed the discovery of rock phosphate at Dunnellon, in Marion County, led to similar finds in all the western counties, from Talahassee to a few miles north of Port Tampa. These discoveries gave rise to the idea that millions and millions of acres contained solid beds of high-testing phosphate, needing only the pick and shovel to turn them into gold. The careful and conscientious investigations that were made as soon as mining operations were entered into, quickly proved the fallacy of this delusive theory, and it was found that even the best deposits were extremely capricious in their formation, and that the phosphate could not be extracted as easily as was originally anticipated.

The phosphate occurs in a series of pockets, and also in drifts, and is covered by an overburden of sand and clay of a thickness varying from a few inches to many feet. Sometimes the rock crops out on the surface, and in certain localities these outcrops comprise an area of about a quarter of an acre of nearly solid rock. The contents of these pockets are sand, clay, flints and sandstone, rough and jagged pieces of phosphate rock, soft phosphate, and phosphate bowlders. The bowlders, instead of being smooth, as the name would naturally imply, are irregular masses of rock, with a rough surface, weighing from a few pounds up to many hundreds of tons. In the larger bowlders there are jagged interstices, filled with sand and clay.

The question as to whether a pocket or deposit is worth exploiting depends upon the proportion of its various ingredients, and the ordinary method of examination by the sinking of a few pits is apt to be most misleading. In order to get a real knowledge of the value or contents of a property it is advisable to cut long ditches and cross trenches, for pitting does not sufficiently reveal the nature of a deposit.

DESCRIPTION OF THE ROCK PHOSPHATE.

The phosphate rock itself is found in a variety of types, which have been grouped and classified as follows by Dr. N. A. Pratt, who kindly placed his classification at our disposal.

1st. THE LAMINATED TYPE. Hard bowlders or fragments thereof, more or less distinctly compacted in layers, sometimes with interstices between the laminations, filled with sand or clay, or else empty, sometimes compact and solid, but in all cases the laminations can be distinctly traced on the fractured edges, and are curved concentrically or spirally around a central point, like the leaves of a head of lettuce, except that the laminations are continuous. In a small bowlder the curvature is distinctly traced on the fractured edges. On a large one the curvature may scarcely be detected, and the laminations appear as plates or slabs.

The colour is brown, amber, grey or white, but generally of one colour from the same locality; they all have a coarse, harsh, hackly fracture.

The average composition of this type, whatever the colour or where found is practically the same; an average of eighteen samples of this grade analysed, yields (excluding sand) :—

	Average.	Purest Sample
Lime Carbonate	7.53	7.46
Combined Water and Organic Matter ..	3.23	2.50
Alumina and Oxide Iron	3.21	.60
Lime Phosphate	80.88	84.93
Sand and Insoluble	—	.10

2nd. THE CONCHOIDAL TYPE. Hard bowlder, generally smooth, sometimes polished exterior, solid and massive within. The fracture is smooth and conchoidal, like the interior of a conch shell, colour cream, white or light, sometimes intricately banded with irregular or broken streaks of darker colour. Its average composition computed from sixteen analyses is, when sand free:—

	Average.		Purest Sample.
Lime Carbonate	6.25	..	5.75
Combined Water	4.10	..	4.10
Alumina and Oxide Iron ..	2.15	..	1.28
Phosphate of Lime	83.53	..	86.32
Silicic Acid combined ..	1.60	..	1.75

3rd. THE WEDGEWOOD TYPE is bowlder-like, has a semi-conchoidal fracture that looks like Wedgewood or semi-porcelain ware—it is dry and rough to the touch, brittle, and rings under the hammer. White and cream colour generally, sometimes stained and spotted. The tough, white, rainpitted rock, type 5, may be included here (see type 5). Its average composition computed from twenty analyses is, freed from sand :—

	Average.	Best Sample.
Lime Carbonate	6.43	Not estimated.
Combined Water	3.85	3.85
Alumina and Oxide Iron.. ..	2.23	3.44
Lime Phosphate	83.71	86.44
Silicic Acid..	—	2.10

4th. THE OREOLE TYPE.—This is a soft mass occurring in layers, irregular strata or masses, sometimes of several feet thickness and considerable area. It is perhaps the widest disseminated and most abundant of all the types. Pure, it is chalk white in colour, soft and satin-like in feeling. It is very porous and light when dry, and smooth and fine as pearl powder ; when mixed or wetted it holds from 30 to 40 per cent. of water, works under the fingers to a pasty mass, easily shaped or moulded and dries into a hard cake, friable but of considerable tenacity. When subjected to heat in either its natural or moulded state it becomes tough, resists abrasion and loses more or less of its smooth feeling ; it does not shrink in bulk nor crack, nor is it restored to its former condition by soaking in water.

It is almost free from sand and grit, but contains alumina. It invariably occurs under and around the bowlders and extends laterally beyond them, and underlies tracts of land where no bowlders are found. Sometimes it is harder and heavier than described, but having similar composition both kinds are classed together. In its pure state it is unfortunately closely associated with intervening beds, or layers, or pockets of pure white sand and clay, or both, which is difficult to separate, and the grade is reduced thereby.

Analysis of a pure sample yields :—

	From Augusta Mines.	From Jordan's.
Combined Water	5.60	2.01
Lime Carbonate	2.68	4.55
Alumina and Oxide Iron	2.30	12.60
Lime Phosphate	87.64	78.10
Insoluble Silica	.75	2.75

5th. Another type is as white as Oreole, but is in ledges or bowlders, is very tough, resists fracture, though sometimes soft and smooth to the touch. It is compact and heavy. On exposed surfaces it appears deeply pitted as if by rain drops, but probably due to growth of a species of lichen. Along with it occurs rock of the Wedgewood type, and as their compositions are so nearly the same, I think best to class it under that head or type, and call it " Wedgewood " too, for the present, at least.

6th. THE FOSSIL TYPE, so called from the fossil impressions contained, and from the cavities of ⅛ to ¾ of an inch. This fossil, called Orbitoides, accompanies the nummullite in all its nummullitic limestone, and in this state is a characteristic fossil of a sand rock that overlies the prevailing lime rock, and which is *not* a sponge flint rock. It is of good quality, hard bowlder, brown in colour, breaks in all directions easily, exposing the cavities just mentioned. The fractured parts, very harsh and sandy in one piece, more smooth in another; in any case the cavities will identify the type. It resembles sand rock so closely that it might be rejected in mining. Analysis of the roughest and most unpromising piece yields :—

Sand and Insoluble ..	2.95
Alumina and Ferric Oxide	3.65
Lime Carbonate.. ..	4.40
Phosphoric Acid ..	36.32
Bone Phosphate Lime ..	79.43
Lime	48.72

7th. RIVER ROCK TYPE consists of either or all of the above types, except the Oreole, all darkened even to blackness by the staining action of the water and mud, and exclusion of air. It is sometimes blue, sometimes pink and even green on the surface. They seem more massive and heavy than any of the other types. The percentage of lime phosphate, in samples from Blue Springs Run, was above 82 per cent. All these forms or types run more or less into each other, yielding mixtures of more or less uniformity, dependent also on the quantity of clay and sand that may adhere to them.

8th. To these types we venture to add another found in the phosphate deposits of the basin of the Ochlawaha River, which had not begun to be worked at the time when the above classification was made.

THE PEBBLE TYPE is found in the drift deposits in the Anthony and Sparrs district, 12 to 20 miles north of Ocala. These pebbles are indistinguishable in appearance from some of the pebbles found in Polk County. They are smooth and hard, and vary in colour from cream to brown. Analysis runs from 58 to 62 per cent. of phosphate.

ROCK MINING.

The first company to commence actual mining operations was the Marion Phosphate Company, which broke ground near Dunnellon, in December, 1889, and shipped their first cargo, 700 tons, per bark "Gler," from Savannah, in April, 1890, to Liverpool. The Dunnellon Phosphate Company took the field in February, 1890, and in May shipped 1,500 tons, per s.s. "Hallamshire," from Fernandina to London and Hamburg.

The general method of mining is as follows:—A considerable area is first cleared of the superincumbent sand and clay, which are removed to some distance from the edges of the pit—or mine, as these openings are generally designated. The phosphate is then attacked with pick and shovel, the smaller bowlders are separated from the sand and clay in which they are usually embedded, the larger ones being broken up with blasting powder. The pieces of broken phosphate, which occur both in the soft phosphate and also mixed with the sand and clay, are raked out during the process of excavation. Originally the phosphate was wheeled out of the mines in barrows, and during work hours the mines had the appearance of a beehive, being densely crowded with men and planks and wheelbarrows. In some mines an incline has been cut into the deposit, and the material is brought to the surface in cars running on the sloping track, and hauled up by a stationary engine. A third system and apparently the most practical, is to make a deep cut, using a cable hoist to extract from the pit, and then remove the overburden for the next cut, drill the rock phosphate and fire the holes. This method keeps the production in progress with the uncovering, and seems to us to be more in accordance with the usages of mining.

In most of the mines where active operations are being carried on, cable hoisting machinery is employed. The buckets in use hold about a quarter or a half of a ton, and on an average about 300 buckets of material are raised per day. The contents of the buckets are emptied into cars, which run along an elevated platform round the mines, which are generally about 100 to 400 feet square, and drop the phosphate into the drying sheds which are built round the sides of the mine. These sheds consist of wooden roofs, supported by wooden uprights. On the ground a flooring of cord wood is arranged, and the phosphate is piled on the top to the height of 8 or 10 feet.

When the pile is complete the cord wood is ignited and allowed to burn out, by which time all the organic matter and moisture in the phosphate is eliminated. During the prevalence of heavy rains the sides of the drying sheds are boarded up loosely with scantling. The size of the kilns (or phosphate piles) varies from 200 to 700 tons, the usual quantity in one pile being about 300 tons. It takes about five cords of wood to burn 100 tons, 10 cords for 200 tons, and 15 to 20 cords for 700 tons. The phosphate is ready for handling and shipment about three to four days after firing.

It was with great difficulty that the rock for the early shipments was selected, as nothing was known of the various qualities, and the work in the laboratory was very heavy. Similar looking pieces of rock were found to vary largely in their percentage of phosphate and of iron and alumina, and pieces of white sand rock were often mistaken for phosphate; in fact the whole business of selection was a puzzle to even the longest heads.

The question of main importance in rock mining is the proportion of first quality phosphate (*i.e.*, rock testing 75 per cent. of phosphate and upwards, with less than 4 per cent. of iron and alumina) to the total quantity of cubic yards to be removed. Careful calculation shows that about 15 per cent. is the maximum proportion of bowlder phosphate produced from the whole mass excavated, including overburden. The average of prime rock mined, exclusive of overburden, may be taken to be about 25 per cent., the remainder being soft phosphate, clay, sand and sandstone and flints. Sometimes in a good pit an average of 40 per cent. has been reached, but taking the good with the bad, the usual percentage will not exceed 25 per cent.

In some mines there is as much as 50 per cent. of soft phosphate, in others this material does not appear. This soft phosphate is evidently the detritus of the bowlders, probably worn off before the bowlders had reached their present degree of hardness, and though it has very little sand mixed with it, yet as it is usually surrounded by both sand and clay, it is not possible to extract it in its pure condition. There are two qualities of this, according to the admixture of deleterious elements, the first running from 70 to 78 per cent., the second 65 per cent. and upwards, but the percentage of iron and alumina is excessive. It appears, however, that there is a market for this material, and small shipments have been made both to Europe and the United States.

Mixed up with this soft phosphate, or mixed with the sand and clay in those deposits which are free from soft phosphate, there is a good proportion of small pieces of hard rock phosphate. In the earlier days little attention was paid to this, but since the reduction in the prices obtained for phosphate, miners are increasing their production by at least 50 to 100 per cent. by saving this material, the test of which is about 76 per cent., with 3 to 4 per cent. of iron and alumina. There are places where this broken phosphate occurs, together with small bowlders, in the form of a sandy drift along the banks of the Withlacoochee River, where the deposit seems to have been formed by the river in the same way as the drift deposits in the beds of the rivers of South Florida. Phosphate is also found in the bed of the Withlacoochee River, mostly in angular pieces, and also in indurated black nodules, which are very similar to the pebble of Peace River, though larger in size and heavier in specific gravity. These nodules are black throughout, and run about 80 per cent. phosphate with under 2 per cent. of iron and alumina.

The Dunnellon Phosphate Company are by far the largest operators in rock phosphate, and, at one time, had twelve mines opened and running actively, employing upwards of 400 hands. About 3,500,000 feet of lumber have been used in the building of their houses, drying sheds, elevated platforms, &c., and the mines are furnished with cable-hoisting apparatus. In addition to the work being carried on in their ordinary mines, a barge fitted with a clam-shell dredge is working on the deposit in the river's bed. The rock thus raised is washed on a barred grating, fitted on a second barge, and the phosphate is then conveyed to the rotary drier, built on the banks, and finally prepared for market.

During last December a further enterprise was taken in hand, viz., the mining of the drift deposit near the river's edge. Here over a good many acres the phosphate crops out on the surface, mostly in the form of small bowlders, and the deposit is covered by about two feet only of overburden. Below this, small bowlders and rough ragged pieces of phosphate are found packed closely together, and the yield in proportion to quantities moved will be very high, probably 40 per cent. Sometimes there is a serious admixture of clay, but in most places the rock is embedded in loose sand, and can be washed with ease and economy. A small trial plant is now running successfully on this material, the process being as follows:

The cars containing the phosphate empty their contents on to a screen over which water is thrown : the rock passes thence into a revolving washer, with teeth and angle iron affixed to the sides. A perforated iron pipe supplies the water for washing. A circular screen is fixed to the end of the washer to enable the sand, &c., to pass out, and the phosphate falls into elevated buckets which discharge it into a wet bin, whence a spiral takes it into the rotary drier. After passing through the drier, the rock is elevated into the storage bin, undergoing a final screening as it passes along. This plant is both neat and efficient, and will doubtless be enlarged to enable this drift deposit to be worked on the large scale which it obviously merits. The cost of producing this phosphate is about 40 to 50 per cent. cheaper than mining the bowlder rock.

Several of the mines working this gravel phosphate, as it is termed locally, have been unfortunate in their selection of plant, the general mistake being too great a complication of mechanical devices and too light machinery, but a short course of experience will soon remedy present defects.

Many of the rock miners have been very careless in their method of preparing the phosphate for market, and shipments have been made running high in iron and alumina, simply because the rock was coated with clay. In order to avoid the shipment of improperly cleaned ore, we are in favour of using a crusher to reduce all rock to a maximum of a few inches only, and screen out the sand and clay, after passing the phosphate through washing and drying apparatus. This is now being done at some of the mines, and will doubtless be the general practice before long.

By carrying out some such process as indicated above, there will be an end to the important discrepancies which have occurred in the results of analyses made from samples taken in Florida, and samples taken on discharge of cargoes in London. It is a very difficult matter indeed to sample a shipment composed of pieces of rock of such different sizes as have been shipped, and the lower tests arrived at in Europe may perhaps be accounted for by the rolling of the larger and heavier pieces to the bottom of the ships during loading, whereas all the fines remain at the top; discrepancies also arise from too small a proportion of samples being taken in Florida. In addition to this advantage, which is of considerable if not of vital importance, the washing and drying of all the phosphate would eliminate the sand and clay which not only adheres to the phosphate, but is also fitted tightly into the numerous interstices and cracks.

It is not possible to give any estimate of the quantity of hard rock likely to be produced from a given area, since the mines differ so exceedingly in their formation, nor is it possible to say what the maximum thickness of a deposit can be, though the fact that up to date no rock has been found higher than 100 feet nor lower than 30 feet above sea level, would seem to imply that no bed is likely to be more than 70 feet thick.

In one instance phosphate has been found and mined more or less continuously for 50 feet, and in many openings where a depth of 40 feet from the surface has been arrived at, there are no signs of exhaustion. Where the larger and richer pockets do occur, enormous quantities of high-grade phosphate will be produced from an exceedingly small area, but the average pocket is extremely capricious and deceptive. One single bowlder has yielded as much as 1,500 tons of phosphate. Nor has the limestone rock in solid form been yet encountered in the workings as far as we can ascertain, though loose pieces have been found from time to time at the bottom of some of the mines. Occasionally strata or leads of large flint rocks, weighing up to several tons each, are found running through a deposit; also large masses of sandstone, and in some cases pits have been abandoned for these causes.

Prospecting has been carried on by some of the companies on a very large scale, and the results show that outside of the pocket formation the deposits are either cut off by flints or sandstone, or else end either abruptly or run into unimportant beds of phosphate so mixed with sandstone and clay that profitable mining is out of all question. The companies organised at the beginning of the phosphate boom have very extensive properties, but the proportion of paying deposits is ridiculously small to the total area bought.

In order to illustrate this more fully we will quote what Dr. Wyatt says of one of his own examinations[*] :—

"An excellent example of this superficiality is afforded by one of our recent examinations, in which the geological con-

* *Vide New York Mining and Engineering Journal*, August 23, 1890.

ditions were of the usual order. The area investigated may be
thus represented :—

5,120 ACRES OF LAND.

Each division representing 640 acres.

Very fine phosphate indications were scattered more or less
all over this tract, sometimes in the form of big bowlders
out-cropping at the surface, sometimes in the form of small
debris, brought up from below by the mole or the gopher.
A local expert had intimated that it contained millions of
tons, and our own first impressions of it were of the highly
sanguine order. A systematic exploration was, however, at
once instituted and carried out, first by boring all over the
tract with a twenty-foot auger, and then by sinking con-
firmatory pits at short intervals to a depth of 15 to 20 feet.
The result of our work was extremely disappointing, and
may be briefly summarised thus :—

(*a*).　No phosphate in workable quantities.

(*b*).　A small basin or pocket of good phosphate, covering
an area of about 15 acres.

(*c & d*).　No phosphate in workable quantities.

(e). Large quantities on surface leading to a very large pocket, covering about 35 acres. Very much mixed up material, principally low grade.

(f & g). No phosphate in workable quantities.

(h). The highest point in the tract very densely grown, big bowlders of phosphate, sandy conglomerate on surface. Fifteen small pockets of phosphate, ending in limestone at a depth of 13 feet."

The total acreage covered by these widely scattered phosphate deposits was set down at 83 acres, and the character, quantity and composition of the phosphate itself as shown by the pits dug, and the material extracted from them, were estimated after experiment to be as follows :—

Bowlder material, large and small,
after screening.. .. .. 13 per cent. of the mass.
Debris and whitish phosphate, soft
and plastic .. . . 29 ,,
Sand, clay, flints and waste .. 58 ,,
——
100

The principal mines now being worked are situated in Alachua, Levy, Marion, Citrus, and Hernando Counties, and though the proportion of good deposits to the total area in which phosphate is found, is merely fractional, yet there is beyond doubt an enormous quantity of available phosphate which can be cheaply and profitably mined, and the likely demands of the market cannot make any appreciable difference in the sources of supply.

ANALYSIS OF ROCK PHOSPHATE.

Turning now to the question of the analysis of Florida rock phosphate, and taking samples right and left without any selection, it is difficult to imagine a greater incongruity and apparent contradiction of results. Samples which closely resemble each other give results as divergent as the poles, and the collector can range his samples from tests of pure carbonate of lime up to 90 per cent. of phosphate. The percentage of phosphoric acid though in itself of vital primary importance, must only be considered in conjunction with the question of the proportion of iron and alumina. A few months after the commencement of the development of Florida phosphate, vague rumours were floated about that the phosphates of Florida were phosphates of alumina, and though there seemed to be adequate reason for certain apprehensiveness on this score, there can now be no doubt whatever that the rock phosphate is a genuinely good marketable and workable phosphate when properly prepared. There are of course places where the iron and alumina runs excessively high, and in one instance 23 samples taken from a property, the purchase of which was being seriously entertained, gave 19 per cent. of phosphate of iron and alumina.

There is a point, however, that seems to us to have been overlooked by most of the companies mining, and that is the distinction between phosphates of iron and alumina and silicates of iron and alumina ; in other words it is advisable to ascertain the form in which the iron and alumina is combined. Experiments prove that if the average piece of phosphate is broken up into small fragments, and then carefully washed and screened, the analysis of the washed sample will show a much smaller percentage of iron and alumina than the unwashed ore. This proves the benefit to be derived by crushing, washing and drying and screening all phosphate as recommended previously.

ANALYSIS OF CARGO FROM
DUNNELLON DISTRICT.

The following analyses may be taken as fairly representing a good average shipment :—

	A. Sibson.			Aug. Voelcker & Sons.		B. Dyer.
Phosphoric Acid	36.80	..	..	36.63	..	36.73
Lime	51.20	..	..	49.08	..	50.06
Oxide of Iron	.52	..	..	.74		.70
Alumina	1.73	..	..	1.60		
Insoluble	3.90	..	..	3.39		
Undetermined	5.85	..	..	7.93	.. ..	6.46
		Organic matter and water of combination }		.63 Organic matter and water of combination }		1.32
	100.00			100.00		100.00
Equivalent to Tribasic } Phosphate of Lime }	80.33			79.97		80.18

ANALYSIS OF CARGO OF ROCK PHOSPHATE.

FROM PEMBERTON FERRY DISTRICT, HERNANDO COUNTY.

	Augustus Voelcker & Sons.			Bernard Dyer.	
Moisture in fine sample dried at 212° Fah.	00.00	0.00	0.00	00.00	00.00
Organic Matter and Water of Combination	1.39	.90	.90	1.36	.98
Phosphoric Acid	35.11	35.39	35.40	35.57	35.79
Lime	47.07	47.54	47.27	47.09	47.40
Oxide of Iron	.65	.75	.75	.81	
Alumina	1.49	1.29	1.71	1.97 }	7.33
Magnesia	.26)	5.36	5.65	3.57 }	
Carbonic Acid, &c.	5.54)			11.48 }	
Insoluble Siliceous Matter	8.49	8.77	8.32	8.15	8.44
	100.00	100.00	100.00	100.00	100.00
Equivalent to Tribasic Phosphate of Lime	76.65	77.26	77.28	77.65	78.13
The Rough Sample contained Moisture	2.04	1.51	1.50	2.66	1.45
And accordingly Tribasic Phosphate of Lime	75.09	76.09	76.12	75.58	77.00
Equivalent to Carbonate of Lime	--	—	--	3.36	—

The above analyses fairly represent what the average results of well selected and prepared cargoes should test, but many badly prepared shipments have given very different results from the above.

The following table shows the results of a number of samples taken on the field[*] :—

AVERAGES FROM RESULTS OF SEVERAL HUNDREDS OF COMPLETE ANALYSES OF SAMPLES (SUN-DRIED) TAKEN ON THE SPOT BY DR. FRANCIS WYATT, OF NEW YORK, AND ANALYSED BY HIMSELF OR HIS ASSISTANTS.

SAMPLES CLASSIFIED AS FOLLOWS :

BOWLDER PHOSPHATE	*meaning*	Clean high-grade rock.
BOWLDERS AND DEBRIS	,,	Unselected phosphatic material.
SOFT WHITE		Soft white phosphate in which no bowlders are found.
UNSELECTED ..	,,	Everything that was thrown up from the pits (phosphates and inert and waste matter).

	Phosphoric Acid.	Lime.	Oxides of Iron and Alumina.	Insoluble Siliceous.	Carbonic Acid.	Fluoride.
Bowlders (137 analyses)	34.15	42.10	6.32	5.20	1.80	1.70
Bowlders very carefully selected (86 analyses)	36.10	45.90	4.80	4.95	1.70	1.57
Bowlders and Debris (160 analyses) ..	29.70	38.20	9.42	13.25	2.10	1.49
Soft White (97 analyses) ..	32.50	41.70	8.70	5.20	4.80	1.15
Unselected, total outcome (76 analyses)	13.80	27.40	18.65	31.00	3.16	0.37

COST OF PRODUCTION OF ROCK PHOSPHATE.

Numerous inquiries from the various companies have elicited widely divergent figures for the cost of mining and preparing rock for the market. Some place the cost as low as $1.50 per ton delivered free on rails, others as high as $10.00. No doubt when mining was first undertaken the cost of produc-

---

[*] *Vide New York Mining and Engineering Journal,* August 23, 1890.

tion was very materially higher than it is to-day, owing to the crude and expensive manner in which the earlier mining operations were conducted, but the fall in prices necessitated economy on all sides, and the average cost to-day is less by several dollars than it was a year ago.

In order to arrive at a fair basis of cost, it is necessary to estimate the quantities of material likely to be moved, and the proportion of phosphate to be won, allowing an average depth of say 40 feet. Many miners who give a low cost of production are working on a calculation derived from the raising of a few hundred or a few thousand tons extracted from their initial opening, which naturally would be where the rock is found nearest the surface. The fact that when larger quantities have to be raised a greater depth will be reached is lost sight of, and cost of repairs and wear and tear of plant is entirely overlooked.

After inspecting a large number of mines, and studying closely the methods of raising and preparing the phosphate, we have formed the following conclusions, viz. :—

(i.) That the cost of putting the rock phosphate in clean condition f.o.b. cars in those mines which have the soft phosphate intermixed with the gravel and large bowlders will average $5.00 per ton.

(ii.) That the cost of raising, washing and preparing the phosphate in the mines where gravel and bowlders occur without the soft phosphate should not exceed $4.00 per ton.

(iii.) That the cost of raising, washing and preparing the phosphate in the gravel deposits along the Withlacoochee River should not exceed $3 per ton.

(iv.) That dredging and preparing the phosphate found in the Withlacoochee River should not exceed $2.50 per ton.

The above estimates are based upon a minimum production of 1,000 tons per month, under good practical management.

It is, of course, possible to produce small quantities at very low figures, where an owner of the lands containing the deposit employs a small gang of men under his own supervision, but when considering the subject as a serious mining undertaking, where a steady output of considerable size is expected and required, the matter assumes a different complexion.

GRAVEL ROCK MINING.

In addition to the rock mines described above, there is another form of deposit known in Florida as the gravel or plate-rock deposit, which has not yet been referred to. These deposits occur in Alachua, Levy and Marion Counties. Although the Peninsular Company commenced operations in the autumn of 1890, on a small scale near Anthony, in Marion County, and shipped a cargo the following spring, yet it is only during the last few months that any attention appears to have been paid to this locality. This is rather surprising, seeing that the distance from Ocala, the headquarters of the rock mining industry, is only a few miles, and that the occurrence of the phosphate is more regular than that in the ordinary rock mines.

The formation of the rock mines closely resembles the phosphate deposits in the south-west of France, where the same uncertainty and want of continuity exists, and it is a remarkable fact that the deposits in the Anthony district lie in a formation very similar to that of the Somme deposits in north-east France. The overburden of earth is very light, a few feet only, and below this is found a drift deposit of jagged phosphate, mixed with sand and clay. The phosphate seems to be much the same as the gravel in the rock mines; but, whereas in the latter the gravel is found together with bowlders by the edge of the Withlacoochee River, or mixed up in the ordinary mines with the large bowlders and soft phosphate, it exists at Anthony and Sparrs entirely by itself, and the presence of bowlders weighing over forty or fifty pounds has not yet been discovered. In addition to this, the gravel phosphate of Anthony is found overlying the lime rock, which latter occurs in the same form as the grey phosphatic chalk underlying the Somme deposits : in other words after extracting the phosphate, the limestone appears in angular pyramids of various sizes. In some places the layer of phosphate follows exactly the steep undulations of the limestone, in others the whole of the intervening space is filled up with the phosphate. The thickness of this stratum appears to vary from three to eight feet, when following down the

inclined surface of the lime rock : in some of the cavities
which have been completely filled up with the phosphate, the
thickness of the deposit from the point where it commences to
the bottom of the conical hole is about 30 feet as a maximum.
The tops or shoulders of the pyramid lime rock comes close to
the surface of the ground, and in some instances break through
the deposit.

The lands round the Anthony and Sparrs district have
now been very thoroughly prospected, and this region will
undoubtedly become an important phosphate mining centre,
owing to the uniformity of the occurrence of the phosphate,
and the ease and economy with which it can be raised and
prepared for market. It has been stated that an average cubic
yard of this deposit will yield about 800 lbs. of phosphate ; and
by making a systematic examination it is possible to arrive at an
approximately close estimate of the contents of any given
area.

The Peninsular Phosphate Company have sold their
undertaking to a French Syndicate, and there are eight other
companies in the field, all busy in the erection of their works,
which are expected to be in operation by the spring of the
year.

The phosphate, being mixed with clay and sand, has to be
washed during preparation for shipment, and two different
processes are being adopted. One consists of a compound log
washer, or hollow cylinder, revolving in water and fitted with a

wooden shaft to which strong iron paddles are attached in screw-form. After passing through the log-washer, the rock enters a second cylinder or screen, and fresh water is poured on it from a perforated pipe traversing the centre. The second system is a circular iron washer with internal flanges, fixed in screw-form, and with a perforated pipe supplying water all the length of the washer and of the circular screen fixed at the end of the washer.

None of the plants are as yet in operation, so it is not possible to speak of results, but we think that in some instances larger and stronger screens will have to be adopted before good work is obtained.

Judging by the general outlook, and comparing these deposits with the rock mines, it seems likely that the cost of production in this district will not exceed about $3.00 to $3.50 per ton for phosphate washed and dried f.o.b. cars. This estimate is based on a minimum production of 10,000 tons per annum, under efficient and practical management.

ANALYSIS OF GRAVEL ROCK.

Local reports differ very widely as to the proportion of iron and alumina contained by the gravel phosphate, but most of the analyses submitted to our notice show a quantity which averages between 2 and 3 per cent. In order to produce phosphate which can be sold with a guaranteed maximum of 3 per cent. of oxide and alumina, it will be necessary to give the material a very thorough washing and cleaning so as to get rid entirely of any clay or other impurity. The following analysis is the mean result of the tests of a number of samples taken in the Anthony and Sparrs region and analysed locally, viz. :—

*Phosphoric Acid	36.08
Carbonate of Lime	2.17
Oxide of Iron and Alumina..	1.94
Silica	4.50
Moisture..	2.50

*Equivalent to Tribasic Phosphate of Lime 78.76.

The following are the analyses of the European chemists:—

	Voelcker.	Gilbert.	Maret.
Organic Matter and Water of Combination	0.59	—	—
*Phosphoric Acid ..	36.76	36.33	36.84
Lime ..	52.08	—	—
Oxide of Iron	1.36	1.12	1.12
Alumina..	1.39	1.14	0.29
Magnesia, &c., Carbonic Acid	7.17	—	—
Insoluble Siliceous Matter ..	0.85	—	—
	100.00		

*Equivalent to
Tribasic Phosphate of Lime 79.81   79.31   80.43

INFLUENCE OF FLORIDA PHOSPHATES
ON THE MARKET.

The discovery of phosphate rock in so many places, and the wild excitement and speculation that ensued, naturally resulted in the formation of a number of companies. Some of these were *bonâ fide* business undertakings, controlled by men connected with the phosphate industry; but by far the larger number were purely speculative, and it is the operations of these companies that have had the effect of reducing the price of phosphate at such a rapid rate. No sooner was a company formed than flourishing reports were published in the newspapers as to the gigantic richness of the deposit acquired, with a view of selling stock to the unwary traveller bitten with the phosphate mania. Ocala lost its head completely under the influence of the red-hot excitement which was prevalent. The hotels were swarming with speculators who were selling and buying lands with surprising rapidity. The porticoes resounded with the tales of the fabulous wealth to be acquired almost in a few days. Sellers of stock were narrating the tempting offers they had refused for tens of thousands of tons of rock, while those who had not yet bought their picks and shovels were talking glibly of raising fifty, seventy-five, and even a hundred thousand tons of phosphate within 12 months, and every ounce to test over 80 per cent.

The greater number of people who were investing in lands or forming companies had absolutely no knowledge of mining, and still less of the phosphate market and its requirements. Directly a company was organised its sponsors wanted to sell thousands and thousands of tons before a single labourer had been engaged, imagining vainly that merchants and manufacturers were even more anxious to buy than they were themselves to sell. Other companies had no working capital, and were endeavouring to make large sales in order to borrow money on the security of the contract and of the buyers' names. Each company had so many officers with their special friends and agents, and a dozen different people were offering the same phosphate for sale. Besides this there were plenty of speculative operators making large offers, hoping to secure the material at a lower figure after making sure of a buyer.

It so happened that at the particular time when these offers were coming forward (*i.e.*, the summer months of 1890) the European market was prepared to receive large additional quantities of phosphate without prices being materially lowered.

In order to understand the feeling of the market at that time it is necessary to look back a few years in the history of the prices and consumption of phosphate in Europe.

In the summer of 1887 South Carolina phosphates (the barometer of the phosphate market) reached the lowest price they have ever touched, falling as low as $6\frac{1}{2}$d. per unit; freights were of course very cheap, but phosphate was being shipped from South Carolina at prices below the actual cost of produc-

tion. That year the Somme (France) phosphate fields (discovered the previous summer) began to produce, and though at
first no large quantities were supposed to exist, yet before the
end of the year it was known that this was one of the most
important phosphate deposits ever discovered, close at hand
and with easy facilities of production. Added to this came the
introduction of ground basic slag as a fertiliser, and the general
outlook appeared very gloomy, for these two new sources of
supply meant an addition of 200,000 tons of phosphate and
300,000 tons of basic slag on the top of a weak market with
abnormally low prices. Trade, however, was beginning to
expand, and a wonderful increase in the consumption of
phosphatic manures was being developed in Southern Germany
and in France, and by the summer of 1890 there was an
increase in the yearly consumption of phosphatic manures in
Europe of over 1,000,000 tons. No fresh sources of supply
(excepting the deposits of low-testing phosphate at Liège) had
been heard of. Rumours were current that the Somme production was to decrease very rapidly: large quantities of Carolina
river rock previously shipped to Europe were being retained
for manufacture in the United States, thereby diminishing
proportionally, if not actually, the supplies available for
Europe; increasing difficulties in raising both land and river
rock were known to exist, and manufacturers who had been
eagerly buying all the phosphate they could secure were openly
acknowledging their belief that prices would go still higher,
and some of them were themselves becoming raisers and
miners of phosphate.

The discovery of phosphates in Florida was therefore most opportune, and good prices were paid for the shipments to be made up to the spring of 1891. When, however, these large and incessant offers kept on pouring into the market, the reaction was violent, large buying ceased and manufacturers were afraid to operate beyond their immediate requirements. Most of them had bought considerably ahead, looking for a good trade in fertilisers in the spring of 1891. The winter, however, of 1890-91 proved unusually severe and protracted, and when at last the frost broke up, the expected heavy demand was not forthcoming. Offers continued to pour in by every mail from the United States, every broker was offering several cargoes, until at last it was said in Hamburg that cargoes were being hawked round everywhere, in much the same manner as matches were for sale at all the street corners. Consequently, although the first shipments realised 15d. per unit, netting about $17 to $18 at the mines, prices have dropped to 9d. per unit. This leaves only about $5·50 at the mines, counting on a 20s. freight; whereas as much as 30s. was paid in the autumn of last year.

Most of the smaller companies had very limited working capital to start with, and consequently were obliged to sell and ship immediately they had sufficient phosphate ready. Other companies had borrowed money at rates even as high as 2 per cent. per month, and were being pressed to refund the loans. Others again, frightened by the fall in prices, were willing to accept any offer. Consequently, within 18 months from the first shipment, the market price dropped 40 per cent., viz., from 15d. to 9d. per unit.

The Florida sellers have themselves to blame for the great fall in price and depression in the market, for it is quite certain that no such abnormally rapid fall could have been produced by the actual quantities shipped. Florida rock has up to date met with no competition from other phosphates : this trouble has still to come.

The raisers of Somme (France) phosphate being incredulous of the extent of the deposits in Florida, kept almost entirely off the market, expecting prices to rise again before long. Last April the price for 70 per cent. ground (Somme), delivered free on rails in the Somme, was 1.25 francs per unit, in December it was 98 centimes, with a stock on hand of over 100,000 tons of all qualities.

Aruba phosphate, testing about 74-77 per cent. was also kept off the market. The usual yearly shipments are about 30,000 tons ; and, as this material has in past years been sold at 8½d. per unit, there is apparently no reason why the same price should not be accepted again.

In other words, though about seventy thousand tons of high-testing Florida phosphate were shipped to Europe last year, yet owing to the non-shipment of the usual quantities from the Somme and Aruba deposits, the available supplies were actually not perceptibly larger than usual. Buyers, however, were scarcer than usual, that is to say, that small quantities only were being contracted for as required, every one waiting for the situation to develop more fully.

During the end of the summer prices in Europe for the various phosphates seemed topsy turvy ; the following were the quotations c.i.f. London:—

	Minimum. Per Cent.	Per Unit
South Carolina River Phosphate	55	10d.
Peace River Phosphate	60	10½d.
Somme Phosphate (ground) ..	75	13d.
,, ,, ,, ..	70	12d.
,, (ground and washed) ..	60	10½d.
Florida Phosphate	75	9½d.
Liège Phosphate (ground) ..	55	8d.
,, ,, ,, ..	50	7d.
Belgian ,, ,, ..	40	6½d.
Canadian Phosphate ..	80	12d.
,, ,, ..	60	7½d.

In point of fact, prices were entirely nominal; every one was anxious to sell, and no one wanted to buy.

The fall in prices made things the reverse of cheerful in the neighbourhood of Ocala, and a meeting was called in November to consider the best method of remedying the situation. The result of the meeting, which many of the important companies did not attend, was a resolution that a syndicate with a suitable capital should be formed and establish a bureau of information, regulate the output and have exclusive control of the handling and selling of rock, and all matters pertaining thereto. What the issue of this resolution will ultimately be, still remains to be seen. It is absolutely impossible at the present moment to make any complete combination owing to the refusal of many companies to join, and the difference of ideas among those who are willing to combine. Granting for the moment that all the companies were to enter into some agreement, we fail to see how this will help matters other than in a negative manner by keeping the sale in fewer hands.

There is a firm conviction in the minds of many people in Florida that the European buyers have combined to put down prices, and it has even been stated in influential New York journals that the English manufacturers are trying to " bully " the Florida hard rock miners. We quote the following paragraphs, written from Florida, and published in New York, as an example of the foolish ideas that are prevalent :—

" If the Britishers can depress prices of raw materials in this State for a year or two, securing to themselves sufficient rock for their home trade, at prices which mean enormous incomes (*sic*) to fertiliser manufacturers, at the same time planting themselves here as miners and shippers of high-grade, it will certainly prove them to be sharper traders than ourselves."

" Why should we admit for one year longer the necessity of accepting such prices for raw high-grade phosphates as may be tendered by our worthy but sharp-dealing brothers from England ? "

The answer to this, a very simple one, is that there is only a limited market in Europe for high-testing phosphates, and that Europe can supply her wants without buying any Florida hard rock. If therefore Florida high-grade rock is shipped into the European market at all, it must be in competition with other high-grade phosphates already in use, and the natural result of over production and too heavy shipments is a weak market and low prices. The idea that English manufacturers have benefited by the fall in prices is hardly correct, for last year's business was far from being prosperous, and the statement that they want to mine in Florida for themselves is really grotesque. The facts are exactly the contrary, for London has been overrun with speculators and promoters from Florida and from New York, each offering "the best mine in the world " to every manufacturer and phosphate broker whose name they could discover.

Over one hundred rock companies have been organised in the United States of America, and at one time 41 companies were in actual operation ; in December last only 17 companies were at work.

It was stated at the Ocala Convention that there were 47,000 tons of phosphate ready for shipment which had not been sold, so it does not seem probable that any reaction in the prices to be obtained in Europe is likely to take place for a long time to come.

River rock stands on a totally different footing to hard rock, for it is a class of phosphate which has been the backbone of the European medium-testing fertiliser trade for many years past. Price has been well maintained, and there has never been any accumulation of stock ; in fact there has nearly always been a difficulty in filling steamers as they arrived, and the large amounts paid last year for demurrage by the various companies would show an unpleasantly imposing total if put together.

MARKET PRICE OF FLORIDA HIGH-GRADE ROCK IN 1891.

In January, 1891, the price in Europe for 75 per cent. was nominal at 14½d. per unit. Pressing offers were made by one company in particular, which has since become involved and ceased mining, and sales were made from 13d. downwards to 10½d. per unit c.i.f. Continent. During the spring and early summer price dropped to 10d., and in the autumn fell as low as 9½d. c.i.f. Continent. In December quotations were nominal at 9d. per unit without finding buyers, and there is every appearance of a further decline, which will probably close down some more of the mines.

Local prices in April were from $12 to $15 f.o.b. Fernandina, equivalent to $9.50 to $12.50, free on cars at mines. By August there were offers at $6 to $7 at mines, and in November 6,000 tons were sold at $4.50 free on cars at mines, which is the lowest figure touched. The average market price in December was from $5 to $5.50 per ton at mines, and it was a curious feature that several companies who had sold ahead were unable to complete their cargoes without buying from their neighbours, who were thus able to get a little advantage above market price.

SHIPMENTS OF HARD ROCK PHOSPHATE.

Year.	Shipping Port.		By Water to U.S. Tons.		Foreign. Tons.
1890	Fernandina	..	1,330	..	9,155
,,	Port Tampa	..	—	..	700
1891	Fernandina	..	2,180	..	55,084
,,	Port Tampa	..	—	..	12,949

In addition to the above quantities, several shipments have been made from Savannah and Brunswick, Georgia, amounting to about 8,000 tons. Most of the rock phosphate has been carried by the Florida, Central and Peninsular Railroad to the eastern ports, the shipments from the Pemberton Ferry district are made over the South Florida Railroad to Port Tampa. A new extension of this latter railroad is now being built to Dunnellon. Railroad freights from most rock centres to Fernandina and shipping expenses at the port average about $2.50 per ton, from Pemberton Ferry to Port Tampa about $1.25 per ton.

At the loading docks at Fernandina, where two large or three small steamers can load at one time, there are 18 to 26 feet of water. The loading costs 25 cents per ton, and no hoisting by the steamer is required. Pilotage varies from $80 for 16 feet draft to $92.50 for a draft of $18\frac{1}{2}$ feet. Depth of water on the bar at low tide is $11\frac{1}{4}$ feet, and tide rises $7\frac{1}{2}$ to 8 feet. The Florida, Central and Peninsular Railroad have built a loading elevator which is at present in an experimental stage only, but quick dispatch is given by manual labour. There are no port dues.

At Jacksonville there are 18 to 20 feet of water alongside the wharves. Average depth of water at the bar at low tide is 13½ feet, with 17½ feet at high tide. Pilotage is charged at $3 per foot. There are no harbour dues.

At Port Tampa there is a depth of 30 feet of water at the pier and 21 feet at the bar at low water. Pilotage costs $2.50 per foot, trimming 20 cents per ton, wharfage and loading 50 cents per ton. Great alterations are going to be made at this port, and ultimately eight steamers at least will be able to receive the cargoes simultaneously. There are no port dues.

The following is a list * of the Companies which shipped one or more cargoes during 1891 to Europe :—

Name of Company.	Mines at	County.	Capital.
Dunnellon Phosphate Co.	Dunnellon	Marion	$1,200,000
Marion Phosphate Co.	,,	,,	5,000,000
Sterling Phosphate Co.	Pemberton Ferry	Hernando	3,000,000
Netherlands Phosphate Co.	Pemberton Ferry	,,	—
Ocala and Blue River Phosphate Co.	Dunnellon	Marion	3,000,000
Withlacoochee Phosphate Co.	Cove Bend	Citrus	400,000
Standard Phosphate Co	Archer	Alachua	2,000,000
Albion Phosphate Co.	Gainesville	,,	300,000
International Phosphate Co.	Dunnellon	Marion	—
Peninsular Phosphate Co.	Anthony	,,	200,000
Florida Phosphate Co.	—	Citrus	210,000
Stonewall Phosphate Co.	—	—	500,000
Glenn Alice Phosphate Co.	Bay Hill	Sumter	—
Jacksonville and Santa Fé Phosphate Co.	—	—	500,000
Itcheetucknee Phosphate Co.	—	—	30,000
High Springs Phosphate Co.	—	—	—
Cove Bend Land Phosphate Co.	Tompkinsville	—	—

NOTE.—This list is as complete as our investigations could make it.

THE LABOUR QUESTION IN FLORIDA.

One of the chief initial difficulties which faced the mine manager directly he arrived on the spot was the scarcity of labour of any description.

Outside of the sparsely settled negroes, there was only the native or "cracker" labour on hand. Trials made with the "cracker" element have shown the futility of relying on this class of hands for steady work. Though naturally intelligent, the "crackers" have grown accustomed through their indolent life to taking things easily; they are most independent in their views, and as most of them own a homestead and cattle of their own, they like a holiday after about a week's work. The consequence is that they are now rarely employed for anything but cutting cord wood by contract. Florida was ransacked in vain for any class of labour, and importations of coloured gangs from Georgia and Alabama had to be resorted to. When night fell, gambling, drinking and shooting commenced, and there were wild times and much actual danger to the overseers, who frequently had to go out with their "Winchesters" and quiet matters down. Firm determination and prompt action soon ended these troubles, which were mostly confined to the small villages or towns adjacent to the mining camps, and now the coloured labourer is well under control.

The absence of any skilled labour was a serious drawback to the pioneers, but when the extent of the industry became circulated through the Northern States, there was a rapid immigration of engineers and surveyors, mechanics and blacksmiths.

The trouble now is the itinerant character of all labour, and the carelessness with which one company employs the hands discharged by neighbouring works. All this, however, is merely a matter of time, and the labour problem—the difficulty of which only those who have confronted it can fully appreciate—will settle into normal conditions.

Some mines employ convict gangs, for which they pay 40 cents only per man per diem, as against the usual charge of $1.00 per day with board supplied, paid for ordinary labour. Mechanics receive from $50 per month upwards; surveyors $5 per day, and dredge engineers from $75 to $150 per month, according to their work. Ordinary engineers, for running engines, hoisting machinery, &c., are paid about $75.00 per month.

FLORIDA PHOSPHATE MINING AS AN INVESTMENT.

A great number of enquiries have been put into circulation in Europe, as to the advisability of making investments in the phosphate mining industry of Florida.

Naturally, the first question asked is as to the price and value of phosphate lands. The answer as to the real value must always remain an open question until results are achieved. The price to give rests upon a number of conditions.

In order to discuss this matter fully, we will give our own views of the most desirable class of investment to make. Taking all things into consideration, we regard the land pebble mining as the soundest investment, for the following reasons :—

(i.) The minimum contents of a given area can be closely estimated.

(ii.) The quality can be ascertained precisely.

(iii.) All the conditions of mining can be calculated, and do not vary materially.

In selecting a land-pebble deposit, the following points have to be closely considered.

(*a*). Location as to available water for washing, and as regards economic use of machinery.

(*b*). Location as to transport.

(*c*). Average thickness of overburden.

(*d*). Thickness of stratum.

(*e*). Whether there is a capping of sand or phosphate rock which has to be removed by hand.

(*f*). Admixture of foreign matter, such as silicate pebbles, sandstone or shells.

(*g*). Supply of timber available for cord wood.

(*h*). Price to be paid for the lands.

It will thus be seen that the question of price is not
so material as would be considered at the first glance ; for
given a deposit of say 1,000 acres in extent, with a stratum
10 feet in thickness, there is a supply of at least 6,000,000 tons
contained therein, and the greediest speculator could not want
more, although of course the whole area of such a tract would
not be suitable for profitable mining. As a general rule it has
been found advantageous to start the operations at or near the
bed of a creek, the existence of which should be a *sine qua
non* of a purchase. On the other hand it is advisable, and
indeed necessary, to control the water course, in order to make
sure of a supply of clean water for washing purposes.

A point in favour of this branch of the industry is the
extensive market for the product. On the other hand, land
pebble mining requires at least twice as heavy an outlay for
machinery as do the other kinds of mining, takes longer to get
into operation, and is hedged round with serious difficulties in
separating the phosphate from the matrix. In fact, so difficult
was this separation considered by many northerners, and even
miners from South Carolina, who came at the outset prepared
to invest their money, that the would-be buyers returned home
saying the deposits were worthless, since no separation could be
effected.

As regards price, the first purchases were made at from
$2 to $5 per acre. When several tracts had changed hands and
companies had been formed, the price rose rapidly to $25 an
acre ; and to-day the quotation for well-selected lands in good

location, with heavy deposits and slight overburden (six to eight feet), varies from $75 to $150 per acre.

Second in order comes river mining. The available lands are now very small in area, and the drifts light ; in fact, there is no land available which contains enough phosphate to last more than a few years. When the river in these places has been exhausted the adjoining lands containing the usual clayey-matrix deposit will have to be worked. Consequently this branch is practically the same as the land pebble as regards investment.

We now come to rock-mining, and though all through this question of investment we are likely to have our views severely criticised, we will be bold enough to follow out our argument to its limit.

Our selection here is the gravel deposits at Anthony and Sparrs, and any similar deposits which may be found elsewhere, such as in the basin of the Suwanhee River, in Alachua County, and the drift deposits along the banks of the Withlacoochee River, for the following reasons :—

(i.)   The area under consideration can be sufficiently prospected to enable definite conclusions to be arrived at as regards quantities.

(ii.)   The test can be accurately ascertained.

(iii.)   Overburden is light.

(iv.)   Deposits are near the railroads.

(v.) The separation of the phosphate is not a difficult matter.

(vi.) The outlay for plant is light in comparison with quantities to be treated.

We now come to the question of rock mining. The chief advantage in this is the high percentage of phosphate, and the small outlay required to commence operations. On the other hand there is the great difficulty in determining any approximation as to contents, and the limited market available for the product. (This latter applies also to gravel mining). The variation of the proportions of rock, soft phosphate, clay, sand, &c., from day to day, and the capricious nature of the deposits are all in disfavour with those who look for a steady investment.

The price of gravel deposits in the Anthony district is now from $200 to $300 per acre; of rock deposits, from $25 to $100, according to area and outcropping of rock.

To sum up, we are of opinion that any carefully selected deposit, whether rock or pebble, drift or bowlder, which has been thoroughly prospected, can be made a good paying investment by practical business men. The Somme Phosphate Fields have given universally good results to the companies and individuals mining them, and Florida can be made to do the same. But to the butcher and baker, the clergyman and professor acting as manager, such investments are likely to prove most disastrous.

It may be of interest to mention the prices paid for phosphate lands in other countries.

In the Somme, as much as $30,000 was given for 2½ acres of land, which produced 40,000 tons of phosphate, netting the raisers at least $200,000 of profit. Lands there are usually sold at a price per cubic metre of phosphate (about one and a-half tons) extracted, for which as much as 40 francs ($7.50 or a royalty of $5.00 per ton) has been paid. A recent purchase of a few acres, very rich, was made for the sum of $240,000.

The Liège deposits, containing about 1,300 to 1,800 tons of phosphate per acre, testing between 50 and 60 per cent., have brought latterly about 10,000 francs ($2,000) per acre, though in the beginning (two years ago) the price was only about $50 per acre.

Canadian phosphate lands, with all the risks incidental to this most varying class of mining, have brought from $50 per acre upwards. A recent sale of 121 acres was made at about $70,000, another of 800 acres at $150,000.

South Carolina lands are offered at from $10 to $30 per acre, according to location, depth of overburden and thickness of stratum.

ORIGIN OF FLORIDA PHOSPHATES.

While it is admitted on all sides that the pebble phosphates of Florida are entirely organic in their origin (as can be readily observed by the use of the microscope), there are very divergent theories as to the origin of the rock phosphates.

Mr. N. H. Darton, of the United States Geological Survey is, among others, of opinion that guano was probably the original source of the phosphate deposits; and this theory seems to cover the conditions of the problem more completely than most of the hypotheses advanced. Others again consider that the underlying limestone rock originally contained a certain percentage of phosphate of lime, and that by the action of water the carbonate got leached out, leaving behind a crust of phosphate of lime. The objection to this theory is the tremendous leaching out of carbonate of lime which would have to have taken place in order to leave behind so thick a bed of phosphate. For, supposing even that the limestone actually did contain 5 per cent. of phosphate of lime, this would mean a leaching of a thickness of 1,000 feet of limestone to produce 50 feet of phosphate.

A third theory is that the upper surface of the limestone rock, being continually washed with phosphate in solution, derived from the decomposition of animal remains, gradually lost its carbonic acid and became phosphatised. In this case one would expect to find phosphatised shells, which, up to date, have not been forthcoming.

Dr. Francis Wyatt, considers that the phosphate formation was due to the evaporation of the Miocene waters [*]:—

" During the Miocene submergence there was deposited upon the Upper Eocene limestones, more especially in the cracks or fissures resulting from their drying up, a soft finely disintegrated calcareous sediment or mud.

----

[*] *Vide New York Mining and Engineering Journal,* August 23, 1890.

"The gradual evaporation of these Miocene waters brought about the formation, principally in the neighbourhood of the rock cavities and fissures, of large and small estuaries. These estuaries were replete, swarming with life and vegetable matter —fish, mollusks, reptiles, and marine plants. They were, besides, heavily charged with gases and acids, and their continuous concentration ultimately induced a multiplicity of readily conceivable processes of decomposition and final metamorphism."

Dr. N. A. Pratt, on the other hand, is of opinion that the rock or bowlder phosphate had its immediate origin in animal life, and that the phosphate bowlder is a true fossil. He does not see any objection to the possibility of a species existing which secreted a skeleton of phosphate of lime, in the same way that the coral animal secretes carbonate of lime. He thinks, in fact, that such a species did exist, and that the fossil bowlder is the fossil remains of a huge foraminifer, which had identical composition in its skeleton with true bone deprived of all organic matter.

These are the principal theories as to the origin of the phosphates, and there are as many or more hypotheses accounting for the formation in which the phosphate is found to-day. Without discussing these in detail, it seems to be agreed that the deposits owe their present position and form to the agency of water, in other words the phosphate is not found to-day in the position and shape in which it originally received its origin, but the beds or crusts or layers have been broken up, washed

together, detrited, water-worn and rolled by the action both
of salt and fresh water until their present form and position was
arrived at.

FERTILISER MANUFACTURING IN FLORIDA.

It is in the natural order of events that the discovery of
phosphates in Florida should lead to the building up of a
fertiliser manufacturing industry, and there are already two
companies in active operation: *i.e.*, The Goulding Fertiliser
Company at Pensacola, with an annual capacity of 15,000 tons
of fertiliser, and Messrs. Little Bros., at Jacksonville, with a
capacity of 20,000 tons per annum. Florida consumes annually
over 60,000 tons of fertilisers (principally in connection with
the orange-growing industry), which are brought in from other
States, and the demand is steadily increasing year by year.

Apart from the local business to be done in the State,
it appears likely that the day is not far distant when Florida
will be able to supply other States with her home-produced
fertilisers. Port Tampa, situated as it is within 60 miles from
the hard rock, land pebble and river pebble mines, seems to offer
special attractions for the building up of a shipping trade. The
demand for fertilisers along the shores of the Gulf of Mexico
and in the Mississippi River Valley is growing annually. Freights
to these points from Port Tampa are cheaper by nearly $2 per
ton than from Charleston, whereas the cost of bringing pyrites

or sulphur to Port Tampa would be only a trifle over cost at Charleston. The question of establishing such works has already been considerably ventilated in Florida, and ten years or even five years' time may show Port Tampa as an important fertiliser manufacturing and shipping point.

EFFECTS OF THE PHOSPHATE INDUSTRY ON FLORIDA.

Early in the last decade the northern promoter had taken Florida under his protection. Land and orange-growing schemes had been projected and put into being. New towns were located, and town lots advertised and sold in surprising quantities. All this was helped on by the extension of the railroads to Tampa and Punta Gorda, and a real boom was set in motion. Huge hotels were built by New York millionaires, and Florida was going to be the Garden of Eden of the whole earth. On the top of all this came "a frost, a killing frost," which immediately put an end to the whole of this speculation by ruining the orange crop ; then came the yellow fever ; hopes ran low or died out ; the population of the newly-built and boomed towns fell away, and Florida became, comparatively speaking, depopulated for the time being. The small towns lapsed into a chronic state of extreme penury. Energy seemed exhausted, and hope of a prosperous future was considered a visionary madness. People who could afford to go north were abandoning their old homesteads; railway travelling was very limited, and the streets of all the towns were practically deserted. With the influx of capital and labour, imported from the Northern States upon the discovery of the phosphate, a welcome revival was at once noticeable. In the hard rock regions there was more wild speculation, but in the pebble districts the growth of enterprise was solid though slower. The town of Ocala, in Marion County, is practically the headquarters of the rock mining industry, and a great change has taken place in it. New buildings are constantly growing up on every side, and each train brings many travellers to the town. All banking, commercial and real estate business has expanded rapidly, and the growth is real and likely to be lasting.

Bartow, the capital of Polk County, which had been suffering from the collapse of the land boom, started on the building of the Punta Gorda division of the Florida Southern Railroad, soon picked up her decrease of inhabitants, and the town, being the distributing point for the pebble industry (both land and river), is once more active and growing rapidly.

The establishment of the two river works at Arcadia, some 50 miles further south, necessitated the building of houses for the numerous employés of the companies, and two years has witnessed the change from a sleepy hamlet to a thriving town of 1,500 inhabitants. In May last forty new houses and two churches were in course of erection at the same time.

Jacksonville, the chief commercial centre of Florida, has benefited very considerably by the revival of trade, and by the development of the numerous phosphate enterprises, which have brought large orders for machinery and stores, clothing and fodder, while the bankers and lawyers have found fresh channels for their respective professions. Bonds have recently been issued for the improvement of the harbour and shipping facilities, with a view of securing a portion of the phosphate shipping business.

The towns of Jacksonville, Ocala and Tampa, while sharing in the increased trade due to the phosphate business, have also invested very considerably in this new enterprise, and quite a number of companies have been formed with the capital supplied by the leading merchants, bankers and others.

In addition to the rapid development of those particular towns which are directly benefited, the whole of Florida has felt the effects of the investment of so much capital within her borders and the distribution of which has been most extensive. Taxes all over the various parts of the State are now collected with ease and punctuality, and the lists of lands sold for arrears of taxes has dwindled down amazingly. Lands, the ownership of which had been long unknown, have again been claimed, and the arrears and fines promptly paid over.

In fact, Florida seems now to be going ahead slowly and surely : there are no signs of violent booming, and the speculative fever seems to have died a natural death. The discovery of phosphates has led to the finding of other valuable resources hitherto overlooked, and the general attention which has lately been given to the State has undoubtedly resulted in a wider recognition of the field which is open for the legitimate investment of capital.

Various new railroad connections are being projected and built, thus largely increasing the area of land available for agricultural purposes. Fresh enterprises of various kinds are being put into operation; in fact, the whole machinery of active business has been thoroughly started on a firm commercial basis.

CHAPTER III.

SOUTH CAROLINA PHOSPHATES.

THE MARL BEDS.

In the early part of the present century the marl beds of New Jersey began to be actively worked, and their contents applied to enrich the poor soil of that State.

The discovery of similar deposits in South Carolina was predicted by Mr. Lardner Vanuxem, who made the first geological survey of the State, publishing his report in 1826; but no further investigations seem to have taken place till the year 1842, when Mr. Edmund Ruffin, of Virginia, who was commissioned to make an agricultural and geological survey, reported the actual finding of the calcareous marl beds.

Analyses of these marls showed the existence therein of a very high percentage of carbonate of lime (varying from 60 to 95 per cent.), and the marling of lands was most energetically recommended by Mr. Ruffin, and also by Professor Tuomey, who succeeded him in the following year, and published a complete report on the geology of South Carolina in 1846.

In the meantime Dr. C. U. Shepard and Professor J. Lawrence Smith made the important discovery that the marls in the neighbourhood of Charleston contained 2 to 9.20 per cent. of phosphate of lime, which ingredient appears to have been overlooked by Mr Ruffin, whose analyses related exclusively to the percentage of carbonate of lime.   Professor Tuomey refers to this discovery as "interesting," and adds *—"Though the amount of phosphate discovered by these analyses brings the marls up to the best in the State from an agricultural point of view, still I apprehend that the carbonate of lime will always prove the constituent of greatest importance."

On the other hand, Dr. C. U. Shepard in addressing the Medical Association of South Carolina in 1859 spoke as follows :—

"In April, 1845, my attention was directed to the cause of the fertility of the marl found in the immediate vicinity of this City (Charleston), and I was led to ascribe it to the extraordinary proportion of phosphate of lime which I found it to contain. The percentage of this invaluable ingredient was so great (viz., up to 9.20 per cent.) that for a time I could hardly credit the accuracy of my analysis .   .   . I ventured to say that I could not subscribe to Mr. Ruffin's reference to the good effects of marling with this material so much to the carbonate of lime as to the phosphate of lime .   .   . You will appreciate the usefulness of a careful examination of all the

---

* *Vide* p. 235, Tuomey's " Geology of South Carolina."

marl beds with a view to determine which have the most of
the precious phosphatic ingredient . . . for I sincerely enter-
tain the opinion that as the supply of guanos from abroad fail
we shall be looked to to fill the vacuum their disappearance
will occasion, and it would not be strange if a few years
hence Charleston should ship more casks of phosphatic stone
to the north than she now receives of ordinary lime from
that region."

This prediction was a most remarkable one, and has
been fully realised, although in a way never anticipated by
Dr. Shepard.

DISCOVERY OF THE PHOSPHATE
ROCKS.

It was as early as 1795 that bones and teeth were discovered
in the Biggin Swamp, Cooper River, but no mention is made of
the nodules or rocks (subsequently proved to be phosphate)
till 1837, when Professor F. S. Holmes found a number of
rolled or water-worn nodules scattered over the surface of an
old rice field, on the west shore of the Ashley River. These
rocks attracted considerable interest, as they were filled with
the impression or casts of marine shells, and many specimens
were carefully preserved, and called marl rocks. These were
subsequently shown to Mr. Ruffin, but pronounced to be useless
as a fertilising substance, owing to the small percentage of

carbonate of lime, which was at that time the ingredient
actively sought after. It appears that his successor, Professor
Tuomey, made a crude analysis, and though he found about
15 to 16 per cent. of phosphate of lime, he considered that
percentage too small, and the proportion of carbonate of lime,
iron and sand too large, to admit of the material being employed
advantageously*. Dr. Edmund Ravenel also had noticed these
marl rocks in 1837, on his own plantation near the Cooper
River ; but, though he called the attention of Messrs. Lyell,
Lieber and other geologists and chemists to the actual deposit
(which lay below the surface and was separated from the marl
beneath by a thin layer of coarse sand), he could never obtain
from any of them any satisfactory opinion with regard to their
history or composition.

Six years later, in December, 1843, Professor Holmes and
some others, when boring for marl with an auger, encountered
a hard substance, about two feet below the soil. The pick and
shovel had to be used, and on removing the earth, a regular
stratum of rocks, imbedded in clay, and about one foot in
thickness, was revealed ; but again no examination was made
of the rocks, as they were identical with those scattered on the
surface of the adjoining field.

* Professor Tuomey refers to these as follows (Geology of South
Carolina, p. 164), when describing the marl beds of the Ashley River:—
"The marl is exceedingly uniform with the exception of about two or
three feet of the surface, which is composed of irregular and water-worn
fragments of marl-stone. These are so scattered over the surface in some
places as to offer obstruction to the cultivation of the land. At Drayton
Hall they are gathered and thrown into heaps."

The next appearance of the deposit was during the war, when in sinking a pit for the manufacture of saltpetre at Ashley Ferry, on the west bank of the river, a number of oddly-shaped nodules were discovered in a large pocket or cavern in the marl bed. These nodules were supposed by Professor F. S. Holmes to be coprolites, or the fossilised excrements (not necessarily phosphatic) of some of those large aquatic mammalia whose bones are found in the marl and also mixed with the phosphate rocks. Analysis by Dr. N. A. Pratt showed only 15 per cent. of phosphate, which was accounted for at a later date by Professor Holmes by the supposition that the surrounding marl must have extracted a large portion of their phosphoric essence.

It was at this time (*i.e.*, during the war) that Dr. Pratt determined to establish chemical works in the South, and endeavoured in 1866 to organise a company for the manufacture of acids and fertilisers. The spring of the following year found him engaged in locating a site for the proposed works and in searching for home material suitable for manufacture. In August, 1867, while Dr. Pratt was examining samples of imported phosphatic guanos in the laboratory of Dr. St. Julien Ravenel, who also was making preparations for the manufacture of fertilisers in Charleston, the latter handed him a rock, saying it was from Goose Creek, and contained about 10 to 15 per cent. of phosphate, and suggested that Dr. Pratt should analyse it.

The result of this conversation had best be told in the words of Dr. Pratt, who says : *

* *Vide* Dr. Pratt's " Native Bone Phosphates of South Carolina, 1868 "

"Knowing from Tuomey's geology of South Carolina, and from the analyses made by Professor Shepard, that 9 to 10 per cent. of phosphate was not uncommon in the marls of Ashley River, I was not surprised, but took a small sample for analysis.

"Two days afterwards the result was known and communicated to Dr. Ravenel, who was then in my laboratory, with the remark to him that it was well worth looking after. The result was :—

"Phosphate of Lime	34.40
"Sand and Insoluble Matter ..	29.32

"The same day, recalling to my mind the nodules or conglomerates imbedded in the 'Fish Bed' of the Ashley, I applied to my friend, Professor F. S. Holmes, who among all my acquaintances was best informed as to the geology of this section of the country and of its rocky beds, for samples of these or similar rocks ; and being shown a quantity somewhat similar in his cabinet (taken 12 years previously from his own plantation on the Ashley River), which he said were the same as the specimens above mentioned*, I was pleased to analyse and discover on August 10th, 1867 :—

"No. 1 : Phosphate of Lime ..	..	..	55.92
" „ 2 : „ „ ..	..	..	55.52

---

* In referring to this interview Professor Holmes states that he showed some 50 or 60 specimens of these rocks to Dr. Pratt, who on seeing them exclaimed, " I think you are mistaken ; these are not the same kind of rock as I have in my hand." On being reassured by Professor Holmes on this point, Dr. Pratt took a sample of several pounds in weight, which he ground up finely, in order to get a fair sample for analysis.—*Vide* p. 63, " Holmes' Phosphate Rocks of South Carolina," 1870.

" Thus I found these phosphates to be identical with the marl stones, nodules, or conglomerates of the 'Fish Bed' of the Charleston Basin, all the physical characters of which bed had been known and described for twenty years, but of the true chemical composition of which nothing definite had ever been known or published."

On obtaining the result mentioned above, Dr. Pratt visited Professor Holmes again to enquire as to the locality from which the rocks had been taken, and as to the extent of the deposit, and was shown a map upon which the Ashley deposit had been carefully marked out. The next day Dr. Pratt went out to see the rocks *in situ* at Ashley Ferry, and was most favourably impressed with the appearance of the bed. On his return to Charleston he found Professor Holmes very much interested in one of Dr. D. T. Ansted's works, entitled, " Notes on Practical Geology," just received from London, in which a description was given of the deposits of coprolites in Cambridgeshire, which corresponded almost exactly with that of the Ashley deposits. A remarkable feature about Dr. Ansted's book was that it confirmed a statement made many years previously by Professor Holmes that Charleston was located geologically on the same formation as the City of London.*

---

* NOTE.—The exact statement was as follows, and is to be found in " Silliman's American Journal of Arts and Sciences " for March, 1849 — " That Charleston (the capital of South Carolina) is built upon geological formation identical in age, and in other respects similar to those upon which the great cities of London and Paris are located, is a remarkable

Dr. Pratt at once continued his investigations, and profiting by the publications of Professor Tuomey and Professor Holmes in former years, succeeded within a very few weeks in extending the known limits of the bed far beyond the boundaries previously marked out.

COMMENCEMENT OF MINING OPERATIONS AND FIRST SHIPMENTS.

The next point was to draw the attention of capitalists to the importance of the discoveries made and to the chances of turning the same into pecuniary profit. The Southerners, however, did not seem inclined to believe in the value of the phosphate beds, though the Hon. C. G. Memminger, who at first was most incredulous, ultimately changed his ideas on seeing Dr. Ansted's book, and advised Dr. Pratt and Professor Holmes to take great care of it as a means of establishing the worth of their discovery. After six weeks of unsuccessful work in Charleston, money was furnished by Mr. James S. Welsman of Charleston (one of the few men who at once

fact but lately ascertained. The basin-shaped depression of its under-lying calcareous and other beds (as determined in the survey just made by Professor Tuomey) occupies a considerable extent between the Savannah and Pee Dee Rivers. This basin seems destined to become as famous in the eyes of the scientific world as that of Paris, from the number of new and interesting fossils with which it abounds, while those of them already exhumed claim for it a rank above that of the London basin. . . The first ten feet of the underlying (Ashley) marl may be properly called the ' Zeuglodon or Basilosaurus bed of the Charleston Basin.' Professor Agassiz pronounced it the richest cemetery of animal remains he had ever seen."

appreciated the discovery at its true value), which enabled
Dr. Pratt and Professor Holmes to visit Philadelphia, and
lay their plans before more enterprising people. Messrs.
George T. Lewis and Frederick Klett, of Philadelphia,
immediately took the matter in hand, subscribing the money
necessary, and in a very few days the Charleston South Carolina
Mining and Manufacturing Company was organised, with
Professor F. S. Holmes as president, Dr. Pratt as chemist
and general superintendent, and Colonel Yates as engineer.
Some 10,000 acres of land were acquired and mining operations
were begun at Bee's Ferry; and sometime before the close
of the year Professor Holmes forwarded 16 barrels of rock
to Philadelphia and the first parcel of superphosphates was
manufactured by Messrs. Potts and Klett of that city. In the
meantime, a second undertaking called the Wando Fertiliser
Company, with Mr. John R. Dukes as president, which had
been organised locally by Dr. Ravenel and his associates,
started work, and on April 14th, 1868, the first cargo of
phosphates left Charleston, 100 tons being shipped from their
mines by the schooner "Renshaw" to Baltimore.

Four days later the Charleston Mining and Manufacturing
Company shipped 300 tons per schooner "Anna Barton" to
Philadelphia, and its reception there is described by Professor
Holmes in the following words[*]:—

"The arrival of the first cargo in Philadelphia caused no
little excitement in mercantile circles, especially among

---

[*] *Vide* p. 77 "Holmes' Phosphate Rocks of South Carolina."

manufacturers of fashionable fertilisers, and in a very short time after the chemists of that city, New York and Baltimore, had pronounced it a true bone phosphate rock, the phosphate fever became epidemic in those cities."

DESCRIPTION OF THE PHOSPHATE ROCKS OR NODULES.

The nodules are very irregular in shape and vary in size from tiny specks to pieces weighing several pounds. There are also large masses weighing up to a ton, but these are composed, as a rule, of smaller pieces conglomerated. The average nodule varies from pea to potato size. The shape is generally egg or kidney form, and the nodules are all more or less water-worn, frequently contain the cast of shells, and are often perforated, in fact honeycombed. They vary in hardness from 2 to 4, and have (according to Dr. Shepard, Jun.) a specific gravity of 2.2 to 2.5. Generally speaking, the land nodules may be described as light brown in colour, and very porous, while the river nodules, which are a bluish black, are hard and smooth, and contain little moisture.

Dr. R. A. F. Penrose, Jun., classifies the nodules into eleven varieties, differing both in their physical character and chemical composition.*

(1.) A jet black variety, with a bright, shining, glossy enamel of the same colour. It is very rare, and generally

* *Vide* p. 62, Bulletin No. 46, United States Geological Survey, 1888.

occurs in small patches. It contains numerous fossils and shells. It is found in Parrott Creek.

(2.) A brown variety, with a bright enamel of the same colour. It is very rich, and is found in considerable quantities at the Bradley Mine and on the land of the Charleston Mining and Manufacturing Company.

(3.) A light brown variety, with little or no enamel. It bleaches white when exposed to the sun, and is found on the land of the Bradley Company and in many other localities.

(4.) A light chalky variety, containing many shells, and generally poorer in quality than the varieties mentioned above. It is very widely distributed over the South Carolina phosphate region, and is simply marl which has not been so highly phosphatised as the harder and darker varieties.

(5.) A dark greyish-black variety with little or no enamel. It is very siliceous and contains many shells. It is generally found in rivers, and is especially characteristic of the Stono River district.

(6.) A grey variety composed of a mass of shells and transparent siliceous sand, cemented together by a phosphatic cement. Sometimes sharks' teeth are included in the mass. At times it is hard and compact, and at others it is loose, soft and porous. Such varieties are found in large quantities in the Beaufort River. They are often mixed with a much better quality of nodule, which raises the average phosphatic contents.

(7.) A dark grey phosphatic conglomerate, in which the pebbles are quartz and feldspar, varying from the size of a mustard seed to that of a buck-shot. The matrix is a dark grey phosphatic marl. This variety is very rare in South Carolina, but is found in small quantities in the Bull River district.

(8.) Nodules having a black enamel and a light or dark grey interior. They contain many shell casts, and are found in the Coosaw River, and on the Edisto River at Fishburne's Mine.

(9.) A variety consisting of a mass of concentrically laminated nodules cemented together with a matrix of marl, containing many shells. This variety is rare and was found only in the Bull River. It is generally rich in phosphatic matter.

(10.) A ferruginous rusty-brown variety, very siliceous and of poor quality.

(11.) Brown or black masses having the general appearance of fossil dung (coprolites), and probably of that nature. They are hard, and very rich in phosphate of lime. Real coprolites are of rare occurrence.

ANALYSIS.

Different specimens vary very much in the proportions of their chemical composition, but from a commercial standpoint the general average of whole shipments may be taken to be between 56 and 62 per cent. tribasic phosphate of lime, though cargoes of marsh rock run about 52 per cent. only.

Dr. C. U. Shepard, Jun., gives the following as an average result of many hundreds of analyses* :—

* Phosphoric Acid	..	..	from 25.00 per cent. to 28 per cent.
† Carbonic Acid	..	..	,, 2.50 ,, ,, 5 ,,
Sulphuric Acid	..	..	,, 0.50 ,, ,, 2 ,,
Lime ..	..	..	,, 35.00 ,, ,, 42 ,,
Magnesia	..	..	traces 2 ,,
Alumina	..	..	,, 2 ,,
Sesqui-oxide of Iron	..	from	1 per cent. to 4 ,,
Fluoride	..	..	,, 1 ,, ,, 2 ,,
Sand and Silicia	..	..	,, 4 ,, ,, 12 ,,
Organic Matter and com- bined Water	..	..	,, 2 ,, ,, 6 ,,

* Equivalent to 55 to 61 per cent. Tribasic Phosphate of Lime.
† ,, 5 ,, 11 ,, Carbonate of Lime.

Dr. Shepard, Jun., adds :—" In addition to the ingredients mentioned above, sodium, chlorine and occasionally other elements occur in small quantities. Iron pyrites rarely found beyond one per cent., is included under the estimate of sulphuric acid and sesqui-oxide of iron. The organic matter is nitrogenous, containing occasionally as high as a quarter per cent. nitrogen."

TABLE OF ANALYSES OF PHOSPHATE FROM VARIOUS LOCALITIES MADE BY Dr. C. U. SHEPARD, JUN.

	Stono River light coloured nodule.	Stono River dark coloured nodule.	Stono River nodule.	Ashley River Land nodule, dried.	Cooper River land deposit.	Chisolm's Island nodule, dried.	Bull River nodule, dried.	Coosaw River nodule, dried.	Coosaw River nodule, dried.
Moisture	3.68	..	1.50	..	0.10	0.84	0.79	0.57	0.66
Organic Matter and Combined Water	4.78	..	5.59	5.26	0.07	4.22	5.80	4.31	3.75
Carbonic Acid ..	4.68	4.28	3.89	4.47	3.55	3.54	3.61	3.79	4.34
Equal to Carbonate of Lime	10.69	9.73	8.84	10.04	8.06	8.04	8.19	8.61	9.84
Phosphoric Acid ..	25.61	26.68	25.75	27.01	27.11	27.26	25.14	27.26	26.78
Equal to Tribasic Phosphate of Lime	55.91	58.24	56.31	58.95	59.18	59.50	54.88	59.51	58.46
Sand	11.55	12.41	11.77	11.37	15.39	9.06	13.30	9.06	11.77

* Vide p. 75, " Annual Report of Commissioner of Agriculture of South Carolina," 1880.

ORIGIN OF THE PHOSPHATE ROCKS.

The origin of the nodules and the formation of the beds in which they occur have been widely discussed, and various theories, differing very materially, have been propounded. The two most important authorities upon the subject, Professor F. S. Holmes and Dr. N. A. Pratt, took diametrically opposite views, the latter stating that the nodules were of true bone origin, while the former, in his pamphlet, published in 1870, wrote as follows :—" And though there are numerous fossil teeth and fossil bones intermingled with the phosphatic rocks, the rocks themselves never were bones, but were originally calcareous rocks, which were taken from the mother-bed and redeposited in basins, where by a chemical change they were converted from a carbonate of lime rock into a phosphate of lime rock, containing very little carbonate."

His full account is as follows [*] :—" Though these basins in Charleston were formed in the Post Pleiocene age, the rocks deposited in them do not belong to that age, but, in fact, to the Eocene, an older formation. It has been ascertained beyond doubt that frequently rocks or fragments of rocks, of older formations and therefore of greater age, are found in newer deposits of a comparatively recent date. Quartz pebbles and fragments of water-worn crystalline rocks are often seen imbedded in modern clays and sands. The phosphate rocks of these basins, in like manner, have been derived from an older formation of the Eocene marl, or the great Carolinian bed of

[*] *Vide* p. 27 of " Holmes' Phosphate Rocks of South Carolina."

marl, which is the formation of the whole country of South Carolina; is 700 feet in thickness, and extends from North Carolina into Georgia. The shallow water of the coast, with its submarine formation of undulating sand-banks, was then, as now, resting upon this surface of the great marl formation of Eocene; both were below the level of the ocean, exposed to the degrading influence of its waves, and bored into by mollusca and other marine animals. From the coarsely honey-combed surface of this mother-bed fragments were being continually broken off by the waves, rolled over the sand-beds, which wore off their angular edges, and finally deposited them in extensive masses in the great hollows or basins below the ocean level. The next great change was the upheaval of the whole sea-coast country by some geological agency, and the elevation of the coast above the level of the sea. When the sand-hills and the submarine lagoons were raised, the basins contained sea or salt water, and must have been so many small salt lakes along the sea coast, having their bottoms covered or paved with a thin layer of the nodular fragments of marl rock. As the evaporation of the salt water progressed, what was left became day by day a stronger brine, until, at last, a deposit of salt ultimately formed as a crust upon the pavement of marl rocks. And, here it must not be forgotten that these nodules of Eocene rocks are composed (like the mother rock from which they had been broken off) entirely of the dead shells of marine animals, which, age after age, were deposited at the bottom of the ocean or Eocene sea, and finally became an immense bed or body of marl, enclosing throughout its great

depth, not only the polythalamous shells, corals, and corallines, but the teeth and bones of sharks and other fish, and of animals like whales, and alligators, such alone as live in the sea, but no remains of any land animal have yet been found in it. All animal remains obtained are mingled with and not imbedded in the nodules found in the phosphate basins, and this mingling occurred in the Post Pleiocene age, after the elevation of the basins above the ocean level.

"It was in this Post Pleiocene age that the American elephant (or mammoth), the mastodon, rhinoceros, megatherium and other gigantic quadrupeds roamed the Carolina forests and repaired periodically to these salt lakes or lagoons, and during a series of indefinite ages deposited their foecal remains and ultimately their bones, teeth, in fact their dead bodies, in these great open 'crawls' or pens, thus preparing a storehouse of rich material for man's use by converting the rocks, prepared of old at the bottom of the ocean, into the basis of a most wonderful fertilising substance."

The above theory was accepted by Dr. Charles U. Shepard, Jun., who, in a lecture delivered upon South Carolina phosphates in December, 1879, thus describes the process by which the carbonate of lime rocks were converted into phosphate of lime rocks[*] :—

"The decomposition of a mass of animal remains superimposed upon the marl nodules, would cause the production of carbonic acid and the solution of the phosphates originally

[*] This lecture was published in the first Annual Report of the Commissioner of Agriculture of South Carolina, 1880, and the account referred to is to be found on p. 91.

contained in the animal matter in water percolating through the layer. As this solution penetrated into the carbonate of lime masses below, the phosphoric acid would be detained there, and the carbonic acid, whether of the original solution or of the marl, would be carried off. Under such circumstances we should expect to find the greatest phosphatisation at the point of contact ; and such is the case, it having been remarked that the top of the stratum—especially when it formed a floor and has been but slightly disturbed—is the richest in phosphoric acid, and where the marl occurs in nodular masses the rind is richer than the core.

"Again this theory explains the gradual transition from hard phosphate rock through soft rock to the feebly phosphatised marl, which is itself much richer in phosphates than the parent Eocene marl occurring at greater depths below. This phosphatisation was accompanied by a hardening of the previous softer marl masses which became denser in proportion to the completeness of the change; it cemented together contiguous masses giving rise to the more or less continuous phosphatic floor alluded to before, and penetrating below produced curious projections in the rock bed, by the chemical conversion of accumulations of marl which had filled up irregularities in the top of the underlying stratum."

NOTE.— The marl proper contains but a very small percentage of phosphate, and experiments carried out by Professor Shepard, Sen., show that these marls that are associated with, or covered by phosphate rocks contain a higher percentage of phosphate than those not covered. It seems, therefore, that any excess of phosphoric acid passed through the beds of phosphate rocks into the intervening sands and clays, and was absorbed by the upper layers of marl, the small percentage of phosphate contained in the lower layers of marl being derived from the marine animals imbedded in the Eocene formation.

Dr. Pratt accounts for the origin of these phosphate rocks in a manner entirely different to the theory described above, and is of the opinion that they were formed from the dead carcasses, bones, &c., of the millions of living forms which frequented the lagoons. The remains and excrementitious deposits of these marine and terrestrial animals were in time buried in the calcareous mud and sands which eventually filled up the lagoons during the process of the formation of the keys, which in turn became islands and ultimately mainland. The action of rain and other waters gradually washed out the soluble ingredients of these deposits, and the residue then consisted of the insoluble phosphate of lime in the form of bones, coprolites, conglomerates or semi-consolidated softer masses. Dr. Pratt's chemical investigations show that the phosphate nodules have practically the same analytical composition as bones deprived of all organic matter and water, and he finds further confirmation of his views as to their bone origin from the microscope, which instrument he claims reveals phosphate rock which is distinguishable only from bone by its colour, the existence of a few grains of sand, and some undescribed forms probably derived from excrement.

This original formation was probably somewhere in the middle of the State, the present position of the bed having been brought about by the action of the fresh water rivers. The first step was the process of the separation of these nodules or rocks from the marls with which they were originally associated, by the action of the rivers which gradually cut through the various strata, subsequently super-imposed, down to the deposit of phosphate rocks. The accompanying marls and sands were washed out and carried off, whereas the rocks sank to the bottom and were rolled along by the current till they ultimately rested in some eddy or still water, in a bed of fine sand or mud which had been previously deposited. The washing away of the banks and the gradual changing of the beds of the rivers would extend this layer of phosphate in its course, the previously deposited rocks becoming covered with various deposits brought down by the river, till what was once river bed became marsh land. This gradual changing of river bed and washing out of phosphate can be seen going on from day to day, and the thickness of the bed of phosphate is a rough guide to the number of changes undergone.

Professor C. U. Shepard published a short article in *The American Journal of Science* for May, 1869, on the phosphatic formation, and ascribes its origin to the "deposition of bird guano, as it is now going on upon the Musquito Coast of the Caribbean Sea."

Early in 1870 Professor W. C. Kerr, State Geologist of North Carolina, discovered along the shores of that State immense numbers of a living shell—*Lingula pyramidata*—which on examination proved to be a shell containing phosphate of lime, similar in all respects to the composition of bone [*];

---

* NOTE.—In 1854 Dr. T. Sterry Hunt, of the Canadian Geological Survey, discovered that the shell of a bivalve of the genus *Lingula* (existing both fossil and alive) contained phosphate of lime, and about the year 1871, Professor C. P. Williams wrote an article in the Journal of the Franklin Institute on the composition of the shell of the *Lingula*

and with much plausibility, in a paper read before the American Association for the Advance of Science, he ascribed the origin of the South Carolina phosphate to this agency.

While considering the geological side of the subject, it may not be out of place to mention that in 1844 several stone arrow-heads and one stone hatchet were discovered by some labourers who were engaged in the removal of the upper beds covering the marl. Not long after this Professor Holmes, while engaged in his usual visits to the Ashley marl bed, found a human bone projecting from the bluff immediately in contact with the surface of the stony stratum (the phosphate rocks). This bone was condemned without hesitation as an "accidental occupant ;" but only a year afterwards a lower jaw-bone with teeth was taken from the same bed. Subsequently events and discoveries showed conclusively that the first described bone was " in place," and that the beds of the Post-

pyramidata, found in Beaufort River, N.C. The following are the analyses of the shell and of the *Os innominatum*, made by Professors Williams and Von Bibias respectively :—

		Lingula by Professor Williams.		Bone by Professor von Bibias.
Organic Matter	..	41.336	..	40.03
Tricalcic Phosphate	..	50.340	..	49.72
Trimagnesic Phosphate	..	5.189	..	1.57
Ferric Phosphate	..	trace	..	—
Fluor of Calcium	..	.882	..	—
Carbonate of Lime	..	2.509	..	8.08
Sulphate of Lime	..	.153	..	—
Chlorides	..	trace	..	—
Insoluble in Acids	..	.091	Soluble Salts	.60
		100.441		100.00

Pleiocene, not only on the Ashley but in France, Switzerland and other European countries, contain bones associated with the remains of extinct animals and relics of human workmanship. The European discoveries, it may be remarked, were not made until 10 years later than those of Professor Holmes.

LOCATION AND EXTENT OF THE DEPOSITS.

These deposits occur in a strip of country varying in breadth from ten to twenty miles, commencing at Broad River in the south-east, and running sixty miles along the coast in a north-easterly direction as far as the head waters of the Wando River. The general height of this area, which is about 1,000 square miles in extent, is only about ten feet above high-water level, and elevations of more than twenty feet are few and far between. The whole coast line is cut up into islands and peninsulas, separated from each other and from the mainland by salt water creeks and inlets. The mainland is permeated by a number of slow-flowing streams and rivers, in which the tide rises and falls many miles from their mouths, since their beds, which meander to an extraordinary extent, are almost of a uniform level.

The lands bordering these rivers are mostly of a marshy character, and the beds of older watercourses are easily recognisable, being composed of rich soil, whereas the higher tracts, at a greater distance from the rivers, are generally sandy and covered with pine trees.

The phosphate does not, as far as is known and generally supposed, underlie the whole of this area, but is found in patches, varying in extent from many square miles to a few acres only. Sometimes the deposit is found cropping out at the surface, but, as a rule, in the known and worked localities, the overburden varies in thickness from a few inches to upwards of twenty feet.

No systematic survey of the phosphate territory has ever been made, and consequently not much more is known to-day as to its extent than was published many years ago. Dr. C. U. Shepard, Jun., prepared a map in 1880, on which he marked the deposit as underlying 240,000 acres (about 375 square miles). He estimated, however, that of this only about 10,000 acres contained deposits which were near enough to the surface to be profitable, basing these figures on the assumption that no deposit more than six feet from the surface could be worked at a profit. Since that time it has been shown that deeper deposits can be worked to advantage, and in addition fresh discoveries have been made on lands previously thought not to be underlaid with phosphate; hence the above-mentioned area has been considerably enlarged.

The localities in which phosphate mining is being carried on may be divided into three districts. The first of these lies north and east of Charleston, and extends from the head waters of the Wando River and the eastern branch of the Cooper

River on the north-east to Rantowles Creek and the Stono River on the south-west. This area, covering some 200 square miles, comprises the best known and largest of the land deposits; the rock is of good character and the deposit of wonderfully uniform depth. The Wando River has yielded very large quantities of small nodules, dark in colour and dense in structure, mixed with a very large quantity of fossil bones. Considerable quantities have also been shipped from the Stono River, though the compactness of the deposit has made mining there unprofitable when prices have been low.

The second district, due west of the first, extends from the Edisto River on the east to Horseshoe Creek on the west, and measures about 100 square miles. The land deposit here is not so regular either in continuity of stratum or depth from the surface as in the first-named district, and occurs for the most part in pockets and patches. The deposits in the Edisto River and Horseshoe Creek have been worked extensively.

The third district lies south-west of the other two, and contains the deposits in the beds of the Bull, Coosaw, Beaufort, Morgan and Broad Rivers, as well as Chisolm's and Williman's Islands. This is *par excellence* the home of the river mining industry, though Chisolm's and Williman's Islands are virtually land deposits. A rough measurement of the area of this region is about 75 square miles.

These deposits must be divided into two classes, *i.e.*, the deposits underlying the land and those found in the beds of the rivers.

LAND PHOSPHATE.

DESCRIPTION OF STRATUM, AND YIELD PER ACRE.

The formation in which the land deposits occur is described by Dr. C. U. Shepard, Jun.,[*] as consisting of the following :—

(i.) Soil and subsoil : a few inches to a foot in depth.

(ii.) A light coloured siliceous clay, iron-stained in places containing much fine transparent sand and minute scales of silvery mica, with a little calcareous matter, one foot or more in thickness.

(iii.) A blue clayey marl, probably altered marsh mud, containing fragments of shells. Thickness, about two feet. NOTE.—This is wanting in the beds nearer the surface.

(iv.) A thin layer of coarse sand one to three inches in thickness.

(v.) The phosphate nodules in either a loose siliceous or a tenacious bluish or rich buff-coloured argillaceous marl, frequently accompanied with abundant fossil bones and teeth. The upper nodules are often harder, the lower softer, and at some land localities exhibit a gradual transition by loss of cohesion and decrease of phosphatic contents, into

(vi.) A marl highly phosphatic towards the rock bed, and occasionally containing 20 to 30 per cent. of phosphates, but at a depth of a few inches containing only 10 to 20 per cent. of these constituents.

* *Vide* p. 86, Report of Commissioner of Agriculture of South Carolina, 1880.

(vii.) Argillaceous (clayey) or Arenaceous (sandy) marls containing 7 to 10 per cent. of phosphates.

The thickness of the phosphate-bearing stratum varies from a few inches to a maximum of 5 feet 3 inches, which latter, however, is quite exceptional. The ordinary deposit is from 8 to 18 inches thick, and a rough calculation gives 100 tons of phosphate per acre to each 2 inches of thickness: thus a 12 inch stratum would give about 600 tons.[*]

In some instances the yield has been as much as 1,200 tons per acre, and in isolated patches still higher figures are said to have been reached. According to particulars lately supplied by several of the companies the yield up to date has averaged from 600 to 800 tons per acre.

The phosphate-bearing stratum is found at different depths, sometimes only a few inches from the surface, more often several feet, the extreme depth known at present being under the city of Charleston, where the overburden amounts to 60 feet. The question of the limit at which the deposit can be worked to a profit depends upon the market price obtained for the

[*]NOTE.—Though as a general rule the yield per acre may be based on the thickness of the stratum, yet the compactness of the deposit is also a very important factor, for sometimes the nodules are packed together very closely, while in other places they are but loosely distributed through the sand or clay matrix.

In certain districts a second phosphate-bearing stratum has been discovered at a greater depth. Dr. Shepard, Jun, says this is to be accounted for by the concentration through chemical agency of the phosphate contained in the surrounding marls.

product, and when the prices are high the deeper deposits are worked, those nearer the surface being reserved for times when low prices prevail. It is usually calculated that two inches of stratum for each foot to be dug is worth attention.

————

METHOD OF RAISING AND PREPARING THE LAND PHOSPHATE.

The work of excavating is carried on by pick and shovel. The area to be mined is first cleared and the trees cut down. A long trench is then dug to a depth below the phosphate stratum; the overburden of earth, clay, &c., is thrown behind the diggers, and the phosphate-bearing stratum in front upon the untouched ground, whence it is carried in barrows to the railway track, where the cars are loaded for conveyance to the washers.

The principal difficulties encountered arise from the stumps of trees which have to be undermined, and then pulled over towards the diggers, and also from the presence of water which it is difficult to get rid of owing to the flat nature of the country. Steam pumps have to be used in order to prevent the diggers being flooded out, but even with this a really wet day diminishes the output very considerably.

Coloured or Italian labour is employed on the digging, which is almost entirely done by contract, white foremen superintending the various pits. The price paid is 25 cents per pit for each foot in depth excavated, the pit measuring

6 feet by 15 feet, and 30 cents is paid per foot per pit for raising the phosphate; so that each foot of overburden adds nearly half-a-cent (about ¼d.) per unit to the cost of the phosphate.

The works are always situated on the banks of the adjoining rivers, and the unwashed phosphate is conveyed there in small cars, holding about two tons each, drawn by a locomotive. On reaching the works the cars are drawn up an inclined track and their contents dumped into a " V "-shaped trough, on to which a stream of water plays continually. At the bottom of this trough there is a revolving shaft, with teeth fixed in screw form which conveys the phosphate into the second washer, disintegrating it at the same time. Very often this first process is performed by a double set of rollers with teeth, in which case the phosphate passes between them, and the larger lumps are broken up.

The second washer plays the most important part in the operation, and is usually a long semi-circular wooden trough (lined with iron sheeting) inclining upwards. Running the whole length of this there is a wooden shaft with steel teeth attached fixed in spiral form. The phosphate is fed into the lower end, while a strong stream of water flows through from the higher extremity. The teeth keep the phosphate rolling and force the pieces gradually upwards, rubbing them together all the time, while the down flowing water washes back the clay and sand, which are discharged outside through wooden troughs. Occasionally the washing troughs are made square instead of semi-circular, the idea being that the phosphate gets more friction in this shaped washer.

At some works revolving iron cylinders are used with iron flanges attached in spiral form on the inside, in which case the water is distributed internally from a perforated pipe in the axis.

After passing through the washers, the phosphate falls on to a sloping screen, which separates the larger nodules from the smaller ones, which are again screened to get rid of the still smaller silicate pebbles and any sand which may have remained attached : the smaller nodules are afterwards mixed again with the large ones.

The clean phosphate, which, after washing, contains considerable moisture varying from 10 to 20 per cent., is now wheeled away into the kilns or drying sheds, where it is dumped on to cord wood, which is then ignited and burns till it is consumed, by which time the phosphate is absolutely dry and ready for shipment. In some works, instead of drying by means of cord-wood, movable cast-iron pipes, with numerous apertures, are built among the nodules while they are being dumped, and a very powerful blast of hot air is blown through them from a specially arranged furnace by large fans, which produce an enormous heat. About 600 to 800 tons are dried at one time.

NOTE.—It may be of interest to state that the first phosphate shipped was washed by hand, the workmen being provided with stiff brushes.

It is a point worthy of mention, that though the land nodules are dried absolutely, they immediately absorb moisture from the air, and on arrival in Europe the moisture is generally found to be between 2 and 3 per cent. if shipment is made in sailing vessels.

A considerable quantity of undried rock is shipped to United States manufacturers, and there are also some buyers for wet rock in the European market. The rock is sold in Europe at a price per unit per ton, but all local sales are made at a fixed price per ton, so that in the latter case higher test does not bring a proportionately better price, as is the case in Europe.

Ships carrying up to about 800 tons can be loaded alongside most of the works near Charleston, but steamers only load down to about 14 feet, the rest of the cargo being lightered to Charleston harbour, where the steamers complete their loading alongside the wharves.

PROGRESS OF THE LAND ROCK MINING INDUSTRY.

The mining of land rock commenced, as mentioned before, late in the year 1867, and by the close of 1870 there were five companies at work. In 1884 there were 16 companies in operation, giving employment to no less than 3,600 men, with an estimated aggregate capital of $1,756,000. In 1891 there were 22 companies, employing $3,000,000 of capital. The complete list is as follows :—

Name.	Works at	Capital.
Archdale Mines (Hertz and Warren)	Ashley River	$20,000
Bolton Mines	Stono River	50,000
Bulow Mines (Bradley)	Rantowles Creek	250,000
Campbell and Hertz	,, ,,	50,000
Charleston Mining & Manufacturing Co.	Ashley River	1,000,000
T. D. Dotterer	,,	25,000
C. H. Drayton	,,	50,000
Eureka Mining Co.	Jacksonboro	40,000
F. C. Fishburne	Pon Pon River	50,000
Hannahan Mines	Cooper River	50,000
Horseshoe Mining Co. (Wm. Gregg)	Ashepoo River	50,000
Hughes Mines	Ashley River	75,000
Wm. Gregg	Ashley River	50,000
Magnolia Mines (C. C. Pinkney, Jun.)	,,	100,000
Meadville Mines	Cooper River	300,000
Mount Holley Mining & Manufacturing Co.	Mount Holley	50,000
Pacific Guano Co.	Bull River	100,000
Rose Mines (A. B. Rose)	Ashley River	100,000
St. Andrew's Mining Co.	Stono River	200,000
Wando Phosphate Co.	Ashley River	200,000
Wayne and Von Kolmitz	,,	50,000
Williman's Island Co.	Williman's Island (Bull River)	200,000

The early years of the land rock mining were attended by numerous difficulties, involving the expenditure of large sums of money. The industry was a new one, and much costly experience had to be gained. The incomplete washing of the phosphate often caused heavy losses to shippers, and made manufacturers very careful in their purchases.

At the time of our first visit to the mines, a little over four years ago, we were much surprised to find that no progress had been made in the system of excavation, which was being carried on in the Ashley district entirely by hand digging.* In 1891 steam excavators were introduced into three of the mines, and as this has proved successful it is more than probable that all the companies will abandon their present laborious methods of production : in point of fact they will be compelled to do so when the competition of the land pebble mines of Florida comes into the market.

In order to give a better idea of the economy in working effected by using a steam excavator, it may be mentioned that it takes a man nearly two days to dig a pit 6 feet by 15 and 8 feet deep, whereas the machine in use at the Bolton Mines can dig four pits in one hour. In other words the excavator, run by three men, can do the work of eighty men. When the overburden has been removed in this manner, the rock can be dug and transported by any unskilled labour.

It is, however, stated by some that where there are only six feet of overburden, hand labour is as cheap, as the earth can be quickly shovelled back into the last pit, a great part of it being first undermined and then "caved," but we do not feel inclined to accept the correctness of this assertion.

Dr. Charles U. Shepard, Jun., has laid down the following conditions as determining whether a given bed of phosphate can be mined to advantage and profit :—

(i.) The location of the tract as to point of shipment or consumption.

* NOTE.—The Pacific Guano Company, when in operation some years ago, employed a land excavator on Chisolm's Island.

(ii.)   The facilities for removing rock.

(iii.)   The supply of water, wood and labour.

(iv.)   The quality of the rock.

 (v.)   The extent, depth and yield of the stratum.

(vi.)   The difficulties to be encountered in excavation, *i.e.*,
          the character of the overlying earth, drainage,
          trees. &c.

COST OF PRODUCTION OF LAND ROCK.

Very careful systematic enquiry into the cost of production
at the various mines enables us to place the figure at between
$3.50 and $4 per ton for rock not more than eight feet from the
surface. In exceptional cases the cost of production has been
considerably less, sometimes in like manner appreciably greater,
but the above figures may safely be taken as representing the
fair average cost. That this can and will be reduced by the
judicious application of machinery is beyond doubt, in which
case cost may fall as low as $2.75 per ton of phosphate delivered
f.o.b. Charleston in clean and dry, in fact in merchantable
condition.

PRICES OBTAINED FOR LAND ROCK.

The first cargo was sold on a guarantee of 54 per cent.
phosphate at $14.50 per ton c.i.f. Philadelphia (equivalent
to about $11.50 f.o.b. Charleston), but on larger quantities coming

forward (the possibility of which was not seriously believed in), the price soon fell away, and at one time touched $3.00 per ton f.o.b. works. The average price has been about $6.00 per ton, though $9.00 per ton has occasionally been reached. During the last of the "seventies" prices ranged between $5 and $8.

In 1870 Dr. Charles U. Shepard, Jun., wrote as follows with regard to the industry [*]: "Contrary to expectation, it has been found that few engaged in raising ore rock have reaped any profit, and it may be added that many have met only with loss and failure." It appears that the depression which was then severely felt in this industry had been caused by over-production and slackness of demand in England, where a bad harvest had caused stagnation in the fertiliser trade.

A few years later there seems to have been a panic prevalent in England that the South Carolina land deposits were on the eve of exhaustion, and large contracts were made running over several years. Raisers in South Carolina, however, were afraid to contract for all the quantities buyers wanted, fearing higher freights, difficulties in mining, &c. From 1885 the price declined again, and ultimately fell in England from 13½d. per unit, in 1882, to 6½d., which was touched in the summer of 1887. Freights also fell from 26s. to 11s., thus partially accounting for the heavy difference in price. The Charleston miners had now fallen on evil days, and price was as low as $4.50 f.o.b. In the autumn prices rallied a little, and by January, 1888, a

---

* *Vide* p. 83 of Report of the Commissioner of Agriculture of South Carolina, 1880.

convention had been made restricting output, and prices rose
once more, till in 1891 $7.50 was reached. In December last
the price fell to $6.00 per ton, owing to the dulness in the
United States fertiliser trade caused by the low prices for cotton.

QUANTITIES OF LAND ROCK STILL AVAILABLE.

In December, 1870, Dr. C. U. Shepard wrote as follows:—
" I should say that the total yield of all the known phosphatic
deposits of South Carolina of merchantable quality and
accessible position (*i.e.*, not more than six feet of overburden),
would not exceed 5,000,000 tons." Since that date it has been
found profitable to mine at a greater depth, and in addition,
as before stated, new deposits are being discovered from time
to time. It is really quite impossible to form any estimate as
to actual quantities, but there seems reasonable ground for
supposing that there is sufficient land rock in South Carolina
to supply the market's demands for at least another 50 years.

RIVER PHOSPHATE MINING.

Phosphate is found in the beds of the various rivers and
creeks in the same formation as the deposits underlying the land.
In some of the rivers the deposit is composed entirely of loose
nodules lying in a regular stratum of varying extent and
thickness; in others the stratum is composed of conglomerated
nodules, while a third variety is in the form of a hard sheet

or plate rock from which the nodules, whose form and outline is distinctly traceable, cannot be separated. The nodular and conglomerated phosphate is found mostly in patches, whereas the sheet rock formation is regular and continuous.

The pick of the various deposits is undoubtedly found in Coosaw River, where the stratum extends from shore to shore, over an area about eight miles long and one and a-half miles wide. The water is shallow and the phosphate nodular ; and the stratum averages about 22 inches in thickness. The test of this phosphate is high, and analyses run from 58 to 61 per cent. Occasionally two strata have been found in this river, separated by about 18 inches of blue clay, the upper stratum being about 12 inches and the lower 14 inches thick.

In Morgan River, also, the rock is of excellent quality, but in most places lies very deep at about 48 feet below the level of the water, and is covered with 8 to 20 feet of loose sand and clay. The deep phosphate is found in hard sheet rock from about 15 inches thick, and is immediately superincumbent upon the marl rock, from which it has to be broken off.

In Broad River the phosphate occurs in patches of hard sheet and of conglomerated rock, and is lower in test than Coosaw rock, averaging only 52 to 56 per cent., and the water is deep.

In Stono River there is a heavy admixture of marl and shell with the phosphate, and the marl being practically the same colour as the phosphate, shipments from this river have occasionally given most unsatisfactory results.

In Johnson and Beaufort Rivers the rock runs low in test, averaging only 52 to 54 per cent.   Parrott Creek rock is good in quality, and the stratum is composed both of nodular and plate phosphate.   Wimbee Creek has produced very large quantities of phosphate, and Combee River is still untouched. Ashley and Wando Rivers and Edisto Rivers have been successfully mined.

The relation of these river rock deposits to the underlying strata is described as follows by Dr. C. U. Shepard, Jun.* :— " Beneath the river deposits occur either

- (i.) A grey marl, sometimes in nodules resembling phosphate, with about 5 per cent. of phosphate (Wando River), underlaid by

- (ii.) A white hard marl, enclosing phosphatic grains and containing 3 to 5 per cent. of phosphate ;

or (*a*) A green sand with some clay, and rich in black phosphatic grains, occurring with and beneath the phosphate rock, containing 15 per cent. of phosphate.

- (*b*) Soft and hard marls, several feet in thickness, and containing 10 to 15 per cent. of phosphate (Stono River) ;

or (*c*) Hard marls, poor in phosphate (one-half to 1 per cent.) unless their tops be coated with phosphate rock (Coosaw River)."

In 1870 the Legislature of the State claimed control of the navigable rivers and exacted a royalty of $1.00 per ton on all phosphate rock removed.   A charter giving exclusive mining

---

* *Vide* p. 87, Annual Report of Commissioner of Agriculture of South Carolina, 1880.

rights, for a period of 21 years, on all the rivers upon the filing of a $50,000 bond was granted to the Marine and River Company, who in the same year leased part of their territory to the Coosaw Mining Company, organised in May of that year.

After one year's work the Coosaw Company were in financial straits, having exhausted all their working capital, and many of the stockholders wanted to suspend operations entirely, as the difficulties of separating the phosphate from the accompanying impurities seemed a hopeless task. Eventually the more hopeful element carried the day, fresh capital was raised and the Company continued to work. In the meantime the Marine Company had its charter cancelled owing to non-compliance with the required stipulations, and retired temporarily from the field. In 1876 the Coosaw Company entered into direct relations with the State for the territory previously held under lease from the Marine Company and continued its operations (which were signally successful) until early last year, when the State enjoined them from further mining, owing to the expiry of their charter.

By the close of 1878 there were ten River Companies organised, eight of them being actually at work, and six more companies were in process of organisation. The companies at work were the Coosaw, the Oak Point, the Farmers', the South Carolina, the Palmetto, the Colleton, the Columbia, the Beaufort and Port Royal, while the Sea Island and Port Royal Companies had not yet begun to work. The companies being formed were the South Carolina and Phosphatic, the River and

Marine (in process of reorganisation), the Boatman's, the Island, the Friends' and the Hampton.

At the present time there are six companies at work :—

Name.		Works at.		Capital.
Beaufort Phosphate Co.	..	Beaufort River ..	..	$100,000
Coosaw Mining Co. ..	..	Coosaw and Bull Rivers		600,000
*Carolina Mining Co. ..	..	Battery Creek ..	..	250,000
Farmers' Mining Co. ..	..	Coosaw River ..		125,000
Oak Point Mines Co. ..	..	Wimbee Creek ..	..	150,000
Sea Island Chemical Co.	..	Beaufort River ..	..	250,000

* Registered in England as The Phosphate Mining Co., Limited.

In the earlier days of the industry a considerable area, where the water was low, was exploited by hand, the rock being first loosened by pick and crowbar. Rock was also brought up by divers, even in water twenty feet deep ; and in Wimbee Creek, early in the " seventies," it was not unusual to see the water crowded with blacks, swimming and diving, and vociferating lustily, as they waved their implements around them. Another method of raising rock—which can still be seen going on at the present day—is by the use of long tongs, which are manipulated from flat scows, capable of holding about four tons, two men operating from each scow. A very large force of men used to work in the above manner, and the Coosaw Company were at the time getting as much as three to four hundred tons per day in this fashion.

The general method, however, of mining the phosphate is by the use of dredges, though in one instance a 22-inch pump was unsuccessfully experimented with by the River and Marine Company.

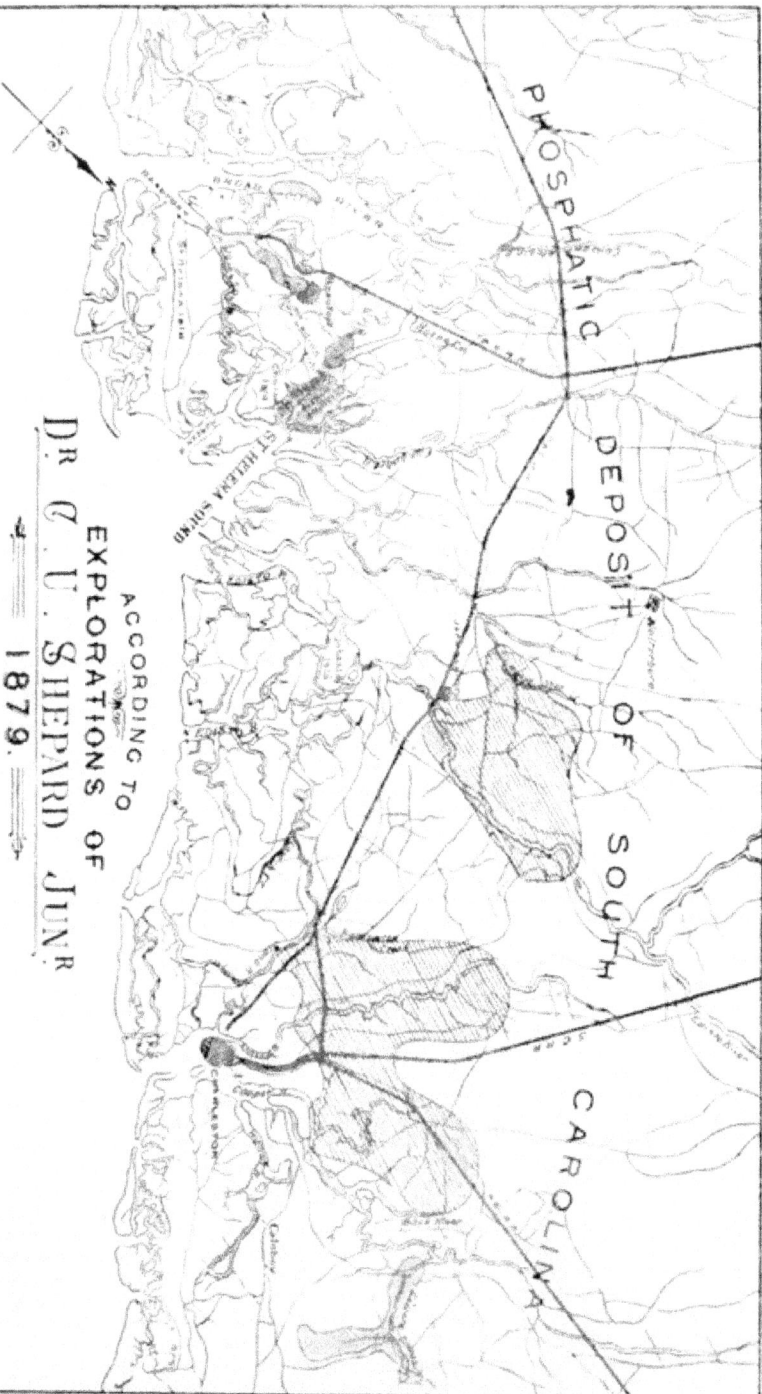

PHOSPHATIC DEPOSIT OF SOUTH CAROLINA

ACCORDING TO
EXPLORATIONS OF
Dr C. U. Shepard Junr.
1879.

There are 13 dredges at work at the present time in the various rivers and creeks. Of these eight are of the "dipper-dredge" description. The machinery, which is fixed upon a barge, held in position by strong wooden spuds, consists of the usual boiler, hoisting engines with friction clutch, and engines for swinging the boom. The boom, usually constructed of steel, supports a long wooden handle, to which the bucket (with massive steel teeth attached to the lower rim) is fastened. When at work the dipper handle is run out till the bucket reaches the bottom ; the bucket is then drawn forward and upwards by a strong chain running over the end of the boom and cuts its way into the stratum. When the bucket and dipper handle are raised to the necessary elevation, a small chain, controlled by the man who regulates the swing of the boom, lets loose the bottom of the bucket, which closes automatically after dropping its contents into the hopper of the washing barge.

Four dredges are fitted with a "grab" apparatus which takes the place of the bucket and dipper handle, and consists as a rule of five strong claws suspended from a chain. These claws are open when lowered and close together when raised.

The machines described above are not built or suitable for working where the water is more than about 27 feet deep, and are better fitted for raising nodular or conglomerated phosphate. They do indeed work upon the plate or sheet phosphate, but cannot do so successfully where the rock is very hard. The capacity of the bucket on the dipper dredge is usually about three-quarters of a yard. The grab dredge is a difficult machine to work in deep water, owing to the current (averaging six knots per hour) being apt to swing the claws on one side and prevent them from striking the stratum simultaneously. The weight of the claw apparatus varies from 8 to 16 tons, and is sufficient to break up conglomerated rock and also sheet rock, where the stratum is not too hard or too thick.

The washing process is carried on in a second barge, and the phosphate is then put on to lighters and towed ashore to the drying sheds, alongside which the steamers load.

The work of mining river rock has been carried on in a most unsystematic manner. This is partially accounted for by the irregularity of the deposit, and partially by the practice of giving a bonus to the engineers for raising more than a certain quantity per week. This bonus naturally makes them select the richest spots and leave the poorer to some other time, so that as a general rule no one place is thoroughly cleaned up, and the dredges are constantly going over the same ground. Huge quantities have sometimes been raised from a very small area ; in one case 220 tons were secured without the stern spud (on which the barges swing when the rock within reach has been exhausted) having been moved. Occasionally a dredge has raised as much as 300 tons in one day, but as a general rule an average of 900 tons for a week's full and regular work is about a maximum. Much time is lost in shifting ground, repairing machinery, &c., so that the yield per year falls very short of the actual capacity, in fact is very little over one-third of same.

The thirteenth dredge is of totally different construction to those described above, and is of the ladder type, *i.e.*, has a series of buckets (38 in number) fixed upon an endless chain. This dredge has been in operation about five years, and was the subject of very considerable comment, in fact of severe criticism during its building in Charleston. The buckets weigh one ton each and have four steel teeth attached ; two at the side and two on the outside rim of the bucket, which latter has the capacity of about one-third of a ton. This machine can dig to a depth of 50 feet, and has engines of over 400-horse power. At the present time it is working on the sheet rock in Morgan River, and being the only dredge that can do so, has practically the monopoly of that river. The dredge is held in position by chains fixed ahead, and cleans up every particle of rock as it works along. Sometimes immense pieces of rock weighing over one ton are raised. The rock is dropped by the buckets into a crusher, whence it passes through a washer on to the barge which conveys it ashore. On the barge several hands are stationed to pick out any impurities and to cut off any marl that may have been brought up with the phosphate. This huge machine, the property of the Phosphate Mining Company, Limited, produces over 30,000 tons of phosphate per annum.

At Williman's Island* the rock, which lies deep below the surface, is raised by means of two dipper dredges, the first one removing the overburden, the second excavating the phosphate. The initial work here was to cut a canal in from the river's

* NOTE.—The mining on Chisolm's and Williman's Island is land mining, and is only mentioned here owing to the geographical position of the islands.

preposterous, and this General Assembly must not hesitate to move forward, and act promptly and decisively.

"The Coosaw River to which this Company lays claim, is perhaps, the best phosphate field in the world, and the lease under which it has been mined for 21 years has made every stockholder wealthy. Their plant, which has been obtained from the surplus profits, is valued at $750,000, or over; and in the meantime, by fabulous dividends, the original capital of $275,000 has been returned to the stockholders, as I am informed, over and over again. When you are told that the output of this Company this year has been 107,000 tons, worth $7 per ton, f.o.b., and that the cost of mining this rock, including royalty, cannot exceed $4.25 per ton, and is believed by many to be much less, you will see that the margin of profit exceeds 100 per cent. on the original investment. The total royalty secured by the State from its phosphate has been over $2,000,000, and of this amount over half has been paid by the Coosaw Company.

"The expiration of the Coosaw lease in March next makes it possible to double the income of the State from the phosphate royalty without injuring the industry, or interfering unduly with any vested right. We, therefore, demand a survey of the phosphate territory, and the sale of its lease at auction to the highest bidder, after a minimum royalty has been fixed by the Board of Control upon each district surveyed. Anything less than a thorough and reliable survey would be a waste of time and money, and this will take a good deal of both. But it will repay its cost, and until we have the data which alone can be thus obtained, we cannot legislate intelligently, or derive the benefits from this valuable property that we ought. This year the royalty has been $237,000, and all of it, except $3,000, was paid by six large mining corporations, whose field of operations is confined to a territory within 20 miles of Beaufort. You will be told by some that this indicates an exhaustion of the deposits, but I am sure it only means that good rock is more plentiful or more cheaply mined there than elsewhere. A survey alone can demonstrate the truth or falsity of this belief, which is based upon the assurance of experts, who themselves have mined in other waters of the State, and as the reliance of capitalists upon an estimate of the value of any given deposit of phosphates will depend largely upon the character of the man making the survey, I have thought it best to obtain the help of the United States Government, if possible, and ask the detail of an officer of the Navy or Coast Survey to do the work. I think an appropriation of $10,000 will be sufficient to start with, and by the time the General Assembly meets, a year hence, it will have something definite to go upon, and can continue the work or not as it may deem best. In the meantime, by means of this survey and the opportunity for further investigation, to which all my spare time shall be devoted, a clearer understanding as to the best system of management of this important industry can be obtained, and the General Assembly can then act intelligently.

" When the Coosaw lease expires, March 1st next, let us open that river to all miners who choose to enter it , allow the

Board of Control to parcel out the territory among them so as to prevent conflict ; raise the royalty to $2 per ton and place one or more inspectors on the ground to supervise the work and weigh the rock when shipped. All the river rock mined in South Carolina is exported to Europe, and last year the demand was so great as to necessitate the exportation of 40,000 tons of land rock, while the price has steadily increased since 1887."

The consequence of this message was, that in February, 1891, an Act was passed providing for a Commission to take charge of the River Phosphate Mining Industry, and on March 2nd this Commission took possession of the Coosaw River territory and made preparations to lease it to all who applied for a licence. The Coosaw Mining Company filed a protest, and on March 6th was granted a temporary injunction by Judge Simonton, of the United States Court, whereby the State Commission was enjoined from entering upon or interfering with that part of the Coosaw River previously occupied by the Company.

In the meantime the Coosaw Mining Company ceased its operations in the disputed territory, pending the decision of the Courts, and the dredges were put to work in other rivers.

On September 18th, Judge Simonton issued the following decree in the United States Circuit Court, adding a note that the Chief Justice authorised him to say that he united and concurred in the order and decree. The full text of the decree is as follows :

" That the grant or privilege of digging, mining and removing phosphate rocks and phosphatic deposits from the navigable streams of South Carolina, given to the defendant under the Act of Assembly of 1870, mentioned in the pleadings, for the period of 21 years from the passage of the said Act, at a royalty of $1.00 per ton became and was, under the provisions of the Act of 1876, an exclusive grant or privilege of digging, mining and removing such deposits from the bed of Coosaw River, at the royalty aforesaid, upon the conditions and within the limits mentioned in said last-named Act for the remainder of the said period of twenty-one years and no longer.

" That such grant or privilege in said defendants has now ceased and determined.

" That the defendants, the Coosaw Mining Company, and all persons claiming under them, and the servants, agents and employés of them be, and each of them are for ever restrained and enjoined from in any claiming or attempting to claim any right, title, interest, estates, or grant under or by virtue of said Act or Acts in or to the phosphate rock or phosphatic deposits in the bed of Coosaw River, in the State of South Carolina, and from digging, mining or removing or attempting to dig, mine or remove the same or any part thereof.

" That nothing in this decree contained shall be construed to enjoin the said defendants, the Coosaw Mining Company, from hereafter mining in the bed of the said Coosaw River, when thereunto duly authorised under any law of the State of South Carolina."

The final decision of the Supreme Courts is expected in March next, and in view of the decrees already passed it seems probable that, eventually, the disputed territory will be opened to all comers.

Should any further delay take place, three-quarters of this year's production will test below 55 per cent., since outside of the Coosaw territory and Morgan River there is but a small area of high-testing rock (*i.e.*, 55 per cent. and upwards) available for the ordinary dredges.

COST OF MINING RIVER ROCK.

In the year 1886 the Legislature considered the advisability of raising the royalty on river rock, and a Special Commission was appointed to consider the cost of production. This was stated under oath at figures varying from $3.25 to $5.00 per ton, the estimate given by the Coosaw Mining Company being $4.25 per ton, including the royalty of $1.00 per ton. It seems to be an established fact that the cost to-day is about $4.00 for the ordinary dipper and grab dredges. It is unlikely that this figure can be decreased, since the operations have now reached the highest point of efficiency and cheapness, and the available quantity of rock is harder to find, and the patches are smaller in area and thickness than formerly. On the other hand, by the employment of ladder dredges, it is possible to work at greater depth, on a more uniform stratum, and with greater completeness; and should these machines—as seems likely—take the place of those formerly in use, cost of production would probably fall below $4.00.

PRICES OBTAINED FOR RIVER ROCK.

The prices at which river rock has been sold have varied but little from the prices obtained for land rock. The general terms of sale for river rock have been at a price per unit c.i.f., Europe, whither almost the whole production has been shipped up to the last few years. The price per unit in Europe has varied in accordance with the freight market, and summer shipments have therefore, as a general rule, realised a less price in Europe than winter shipments. Local prices have been as low as $3, and as high as $9, f.o.b., and $6 has been about the average. Last summer, when freights were low and prices high in Europe, the miners had probably the most lucrative returns ever realised, but prices have fallen again, and present quotation (January, 1892) is about $5.50 to $6.00 per ton, although some actual sales have been made below these figures.

SHIPPING FACILITIES FOR LOADING RIVER ROCK.

In the early days of the industry no steamers were able to come up the rivers, but after dredging there was sufficient depth of channel to enable the steamers to receive their cargoes in the rivers instead of loading in the bay.

At the present day large steamers, say up to 2,200 tons, can load the phosphate alongside the works of the Sea Island and the Phosphate Mining Companies. At the other works the

steamers can only be loaded down to fourteen feet, and the rest
of the cargo is lightered down to deep water in the Sound.
Freights vary from 10s. to 26s. per ton, being at their lowest in
the summer months, and rising when shipments of cotton and
grain are being made to Europe.

QUANTITIES RAISED OF LAND AND RIVER PHOSPHATE.

The following are the official figures of the quantities of
phosphate raised since the commencement of operations :—

Year.		Land Rock. Tons.	River Rock. Tons.	Totals. Tons.
1868/70	..	118,000	1,989	119,989
1871	..	33,000	17,655	50,655
1872	..	38,000	22,502	60,502
1873	..	45,000	45,777	90,777
1874	..	43,000	57,716	100,716
1875	..	48,000	67,969	115,969
1876	..	54,000	81,912	135,912
1877	..	39,000	126,569	165,569
1878	..	113,000	97,700	210,700
1879	..	102,000	98,586	200,586
1880	..	125,000	65,162	190,162
1881	..	141,000	124,541	265,541
1882	..	190,000	140,772	330,772
1883	..	226,000	129,318	355,318
1884	..	258,000	151,243	409,243
1885	..	224,000	171,671	395,671
1886	..	294,000	191,194	485,194
1887	..	230,000	202,757	432,757
1888	..	260,000	190,274	450,274
1889	..	250,000	212,101	462,101
1890	..	300,000	237,149	537,149
1891	..	375,000	197,949	572,949

The quantities of river rock used locally, and shipped by rail or water to United States points during the last seven years, have been as follows :—

Year.	Local. Tons.	Shipments. Tons.	Total.
1884/85	7.500	31,700	39,200
1885/86	11,000	27,288	38,288
1886/87	10,000	17,625	27,625
1887/88	12,000	29,000	41,000
1888/89	15,000	58,500	73,500
1889/90	16,000	49,870	65,870
1890/91	16,000	42,246	58,246

THE SOUTH CAROLINA FERTILISER MANUFACTURING INDUSTRY.

Concurrently with the development of the raising of phosphates in South Carolina there has been built up an important manufacturing business in chemical fertilisers. The peculiar advantages offered by Charleston for the location of mill sites have been a strong factor in the growth of this industry. Situated between the Ashley and the Cooper Rivers, with ample depth of water along both river points, it was only natural that these facilities should lead to the establishment of factories, since both the incoming and outgoing products could be handled cheaply and with ease. In addition to this, Charleston is a good distributing point, being well served by several railroad companies. Savannah, Georgia, also has many

advantages for the same class of business, and it will be seen from
the figures given below that a large business is carried on there
in fertilisers. Port Royal followed the lead given by Charleston
and Savannah, and must be reckoned among the important
fertiliser manufacturing centres.

In 1870 there were in South Carolina seven companies
engaged in this industry, namely, the Wando (the pioneer
company), the Etiwan, the Carolina, the Atlantic, the Stono,
the Farmers', and the Pacific Guano Company. The six
companies first named had an aggregate capital of $2,000,000,
the last-named one of $1,000,000. This Company failed
some years ago but has now been reorganised, and started fresh
operations.

At the close of 1891 there were twenty-two fertiliser
manufacturing companies at work at South Carolina, and the
following are the names of the various undertakings :—

Ashepoo Phosphate Co., Works at Charleston, South Carolina.

Ashley	,,	,,	,,	,,
Atlantic	,,	,,	,,	,,
Baldwin Fertiliser	,	,,	Port Royal	,,
Berkeley Phosphate	,,	,,	Charleston	,,
Chicora Fertiliser	,.	,,	,,	,,
Columbia Phosphate	,,	,,	,,	,,
Edisto	,,	,	,,	,,
Etrivan	,,	,,	,,	,,
Georgia Chemical Works		,,	Jacksonboro	,,
Globe	,,	,,	Columbia	,,
Greenville Fertiliser	,,	,,	Greenville	,,
Imperial	,,	,,	Charleston	,,

FERTILISER MANUFACTURING COMPANIES AT WORK IN

SOUTH CAROLINA—*continued.*

Meade Phosphate Co., Works at Charleston, South Carolina.			
Port Royal Fertiliser	..	..	Port Royal	,,
Pacific Company	.,	..	Charleston	..
Piedmont	..	..	,,	
Royal Fertiliser	.,	..	.	
Stono Phosphate		,.	..	
Wando	,,	,,	,.	..	.,
Wappoo Mills		,.	.	..	..
Willcox and Gibbs Fertiliser	..		,.	,.

with an aggregate capital of about $4,500,000, and an estimated yearly output of about 400,000 tons of manufactured fertiliser. These companies use the land rock almost entirely, the bulk of the river-rock being shipped to Europe, where it is much preferred to the land rock, which is higher in oxide of iron and alumina, and gives a light-coloured superphosphate. The river rock, when manufactured, makes a superphosphate of a slatey-grey hue, which is the standard medium testing "super" of the European market.

The following are the names of the fertiliser companies in Savannah :—

> Baldwin Fertiliser Company.
> Commercial Guano Company.
> Comer, Hull & Co.
> Savannah Guano Company.
> Willcox, Gibbs & Co.

The following tables show the actual increase in the manufacturing industry, and give the shipments of fertilisers from Charleston, Savannah and Port Royal up to the close of 1891 :

SHIPMENTS OF FERTILISERS.

Year.	From Charleston.	From Savannah.	From Port Royal.	Total.
1871	20,487	27,447	—	47,934
1872	37,183	32,922	—	70,105
1873	56,298	56,296	—	112,594
1874	46,263	30,895	—	77,158
1875	49,500	33,187	4,000	86,687
1876	47,381	33,000	12,000	92,381
1877	45,766	45,591	26,000	117,357
1878	52,000	61,500	15,000	128,500
1879	55,000	60,000	12,000	127,000
1880	80,000	75,000	26,000	181,000
1881	100,000	110,000	39,245	249,245
1882	95,000	100,000	28,279	223,279
1883	130,000	125,000	25,000	280,000
1884	143,790	70,000	23,094	236,884
1885	158,136	76,874	33,538	268,548
1886	141,287	82,705	55,527	279,519
1887	131,000	71,844	52,367	255,211
1888	183,000	80,461	59,659	323,120
1889	181,990	85,550	35,000	322,540
1890	261,650	75,000	50,000	386,650
1891	287,975	112,000	51,000	450,975

The fertiliser industry has on the whole given steady and profitable returns upon the money invested, and the last two years have been exceptionally good ones.

PROFITS OF THE SOUTH CAROLINA PHOSPHATE INDUSTRY.

The discovery of phosphates in South Carolina was a boon of which the advantages cannot be too highly appreciated, for the operations began at a time when the whole South was suffering from the terrible straits into which the war had plunged them. The commencement of this new and important

industry planted fresh hopes, ambition and energy in the hearts
of the Southerners, and though at first the actual pecuniary
results were not as satisfactory as could have been desired, yet
the industry was employing hundreds, if not thousands, of men
who would otherwise have been idle. Many of the earlier
companies were wound up, but taking the industry as a whole
its results to date have been eminently profitable. The
Charleston South Carolina Mining and Manufacturing
Company has been the most successful of the land companies,
and for many years past has paid large dividends. The stock of
the company, $100 per share, has generally stood above $200
and been quoted even at $300. The Coosaw Mining Company
has earned and paid the largest dividends ever known in the
history of phosphate mining; one year 300 per cent. was
actually divided, and the $100 stock touched $1,500. Taking
$4 as an average cost for the rock and $6 as the average sale,
it will be seen that the returns have been good, and last year
they were especially high, as rock averaged over $7.00 per ton.
River rock last year realised even as high as $9.00 per ton,
f.o.b., so that the late history of the undertaking as a whole
has proved most satisfactory to those interested.

FUTURE OF THE SOUTH CAROLINA PHOSPHATE INDUSTRY.

The important dimensions which this industry has assumed
must be ascribed to the rapid increase in the demand for
fertilisers throughout the Southern States, principally in connection with the cotton-growing plantations.

The following figures are an estimate of the annual consumption of fertilisers in some of the States, viz. :—Georgia, 230,000 tons ; North Carolina, 150,000 tons ; South Carolina, 200,000 tons ; Alabama, 125,000 tons ; Virginia, 150,000 tons ; Mississippi, 50,000 tons ; Louisiana, 25,000 tons ; Tennessee, 25,000 tons.

In the last few years a considerable number of new fertiliser works have been built and the older ones enlarged, and there seems no doubt as to the probable steady growth of the fertiliser trade for many years to come.

The establishment of manufactories in the neighbourhood of Charleston is the greatest safeguard for the continuance of the mining industry, and though it is probable that the pebble phosphate of Florida will in the future be a strong competitor at northern sea points, yet the situation of Charleston, as regards southern points to be reached by rail, will continue to give her command of those markets. It may be, however, that in a short time from now land rock will cease to be shipped by water from Charleston, or, at all events, shipped in comparatively small quantities, the whole production being either used locally or sent by rail into Georgia, Alabama and other neighbouring States.

River rock will continue to be shipped to Europe, though the wants of Europe will probably be divided between Florida and South Carolina in about equal quantities.

CHAPTER IV.

—

CANADIAN PHOSPHATES.

GEOLOGICAL FORMATION.

Canadian phosphate, Apatite, is found in the oldest known rock formation of the earth's crust, entitled the Laurentian system, which is the earlier sub-division of the Archœan period.

The rocks of this period are supposed by some geologists to be a part of the primeval crust of the earth, solidified from fusion. Others are of opinion that these rocks were formed in the boiling ocean, which first condensed upon the hot surface of the globe, being deposited as chemical precipitates or mechanical sediments on the floor of the primeval ocean, subsequent to which they became more or less crystallised and disturbed. The most abundant rock of this formation (in the region now to be considered) is granitoid gneiss, which is here found interstratified with bands of pyroxene and other hornblendic rocks and crystallised limestone ; these bands or belts being invariably mineralised and carrying quartzite, apatite, pyrite, mica, steatite, feldspar, graphite, scapolite, calcite, &c., in variable proportion, sometimes as distinct veins or beds, at other times as segregated and pockety masses.

No unquestionable trace of organic existence has been met with among these rocks, though certain geologists claim that a structure known as the *Eozoon Canadense* is really that of a reef-building foraminifer. This structure is certainly a noticeable one, but so greatly resembles other recognised mineral arrangements, that its claim to be regarded as an organism cannot be considered in any way to have been established. Further, it is held by most of the scientists that there has always been phosphoric acid in the earth's crust, long before it was possible for any life to have existed upon the globe.

Professor A. R. C. Selwyn, head of the Canadian Geological Survey, says :—

"I hold that there is absolutely no evidence whatever of the organic origin of the apatite, or that the deposits have resulted from ordinary mechanical sedimentation processes. They are clearly connected for the most part with the basic eruptions of Archæan date."

On the other hand, Professor J. W. Dawson thinks that Canadian apatite is of animal origin, basing his belief on the presence of the Eozoon structure and of the fluoride of lime in the apatite. His statement is as follows :—* "The probability of the animal origin of the Laurentian apatite is, perhaps, further strengthened by the prevalence of animals with phosphatic crusts and skeletons in the primordial age, giving a presumption that in the still earlier Laurentian, a similar preference for

---

* *Quarterly Journal*, Geol. Soc., London : vol. xxxii., 1876, p. 290.

phosphatic matter may have existed, and may perhaps have extended to still lower forms of life, just as—in more modern times—the appropriation of phosphate of lime by the higher animals for their bones seems to have been accompanied by a diminution of its use in animals of lower grade."

The general opinion seems to be that the deposits of apatite are really irregular segregations from the phosphate-bearing country rock. Dr. Sterry Hunt describes them as "concretionary vein stones which have resulted from a hot water solution." He finds confirmation of this theory in the rounded form of many of the apatite crystals, which he considers due to partial solution after deposition, and not to fusion as suggested by others. He further supports his argument by the occurrence of drusy cavities in the veins, and of masses of calcite buried in the interior of apatite crystals.

These Laurentian rocks form huge belts which can be traced for many miles, and which swell out into thick zones in some places, diminishing and actually disappearing in others. The general trend of these belts is in N.E. and S.W. direction, and the apatite is found bedded or interstratified with the various rocks, the proportions of which are always varying.

The apatite, which is crystalline in form, varies in colour from a light emerald green to shades of blue, pink, red, yellow, dark green, and an almost absolute black, the usual colour being a bluey-green of different shades.

Its occurrence takes almost every variety of form possible ; at times it appears to occur in true fissure veins. Many of these veins are of considerable length, and in Renfrew and Frontenac Counties, Province of Ontario, have been traced for many miles. The vein matter is principally composed of apatite, calcite and hornblende, the proportions of which to the whole of the vein matter alter at intervals, and the vein itself widens and contracts all along its course. The veins, as a rule, are not sharply divided from the country rock, but blend gradually into it. There are, on the other hand, places where the ending of the vein matter is distinctly defined. The general formation may be described as a series of pockets or beds of various sizes, connected with small stringers or leads of phosphate. Occasionally enormous pockets or bonanzas of pure apatite are found with no admixture of the associated minerals ; at other times there are huge bunches of apatite, calcite, quartzite and pyroxene all intimately mixed together. In some of the mines hexagonal crystals of apatite (which are found in all the deposits) are disseminated in parallel bars through the rocks, in other places the rocks are simply honeycombed with small pieces of apatite about the size of a pea.

There are two main districts in Canada, where apatite occurs in workable quantities. The district where mining was first carried on was in the province of Ontario, where the apatite-bearing belts are found distributed over Addington, Frontenac, Lanark, Leeds and Renfrew Counties. This district is about 75 miles in breadth, and 100 miles in length, and runs from the St. Lawrence River in a northerly direction towards the Ottawa River.

The second district is in Ottawa County, Quebec Province. The belt here varies in width from fifteen to twenty-five miles, beginning near the north bank of the Ottawa River, in the neighbourhood of Ottawa, Templeton and Buckingham, and running northwards through Hull, Templeton, Buckingham, Portland, Wakefield, Denholm, Bowman and other townships. In other words, the belt follows the lands on either side of the Gatineau and du Lièvre Rivers. The extent of the belt to the north is unknown, since the part of the country more than a few miles north of the High Falls on the du Lièvre River is practically unexplored as regards its mineral contents.

Although the districts mentioned above are those in which apatite has been discovered in the largest quantities, there are many other counties in which it is known to exist, notably in Pontiac County, Quebec Province, and in Haliburton to the north of Toronto.

In all these districts the apatite-bearing beds are more or less completely metamorphosed, being sometimes indistinctly stratified, and at other times massive and with no traces of bedding.* In the Ottawa County district the country is wild and rough, and consists of a series of rounded and rolling hills rising up to about 700 feet above the river beds, in ranges with

---

* *Vide* R. A. F. Penrose's description in Bulletin No. 46, of United States Geological Survey on the "Nature and Origin of Deposits of Phosphate of Lime," p. 25.

a general N.E. and S.W. trend. The apatite-bearing veins or leads can be traced with ease over this part of the country, and the richest section appears to be in the townships of Portland West, and S. Bowman, commencing a few miles north of High Falls on the west bank, and running to the south of the Ross Mountain. Here it is that very large pockets or bonanzas have been found, but their occurrence is most capricious.

DESCRIPTION OF THE MINING OPERATIONS.

Although the original discovery of the apatite was made in Ottawa County, it was in the township of Burgess, Lanark County, Province of Ontario, that the first mining was commenced early in the "sixties." The Ottawa region began to be exploited about 1871, and it is stated that the first shipment to England was made in the following year.

In the earlier years most of the mining was done by contract, the local farmers receiving so many dollars per ton of apatite delivered at a certain place. This method was almost universal in the Ontario district, and in fact has been continued up to the present date. The results of such a system obviously were and are, that the various properties were worked in a most primitive and irregular manner. When a good surface-showing or outcrop was found, a pit or open cutting was made and the mineral extracted to such a depth as could be worked without any regular hoisting apparatus. When the pit became difficult to work or was filled with surface water, it was immediately abandoned and work commenced afresh elsewhere. In one property alone we counted more than one hundred openings within a range of one mile, not one of which was over fifteen feet in depth, the majority being only sunk to about ten feet.

This work was usually carried on during the winter months by farmers and any unskilled labour which was idle during the period of the heavy snows and frosts. Although such a method of raising any mineral is much to be deprecated, yet it is probable that these early days and primitive methods resulted in greater gains to the owners of properties than the more recent and regular operations.

Owing no doubt to this abandoning of pits, when too troublesome to work in consequence of their depth, the erroneous idea used to be prevalent in Europe that the apatite in the Ontario district was found in shallow pockets only. The results of our own investigations in the Perth and Sydenham districts of Ontario and in Ottawa County have led us to make the following general description or comparison of the two localities, viz.: That in the former regular stratified veins of nearly perpendicular dip and persistent formation, occurring mostly in parallel lines at close intervals, and varying in thickness from a few inches to several feet, are to be found, while in the latter the usual formation is in capriciously occurring pockets of varying extent, although on the east bank of the du Lièvre River there appear to be beds or veins of greater regularity than on the lands to the west of the river.

The finding of these rich pockets or bonanzas in the Ottawa district led eventually to a general transference of the larger operations to that locality. The first company of any importance was the Buckingham Mining Company, which worked a property on the east bank of the du Lièvre River, about eleven miles above the village of Buckingham. Owing to a fall in the prices of the phosphate market in the year 1875, the operations of this Company, which had but a small working capital, came to a sudden conclusion, and no solid enterprises seem to have been set on foot till six or seven years later, private individuals having continued the various workings in the meantime. In the years 1883 and 1884 several joint stock companies were organised, and the du Lièvre River became the centre of much mining activity.

In order to furnish a better idea of the industry as a whole, it will be well to give a description of the various mines which have been opened and the methods by which they have been worked.

The village of Buckingham, situated three miles north of the main line of the Canadian Pacific Railroad, at a point about twenty miles east of Ottawa, is practically the centre of the Canadian phosphate mining industry.

It is here that the scows unload the phosphate taken on board at the riverside wharves of the various mining undertakings of the du Lièvre River district. A branch line from Buckingham Station (on the C.P.R.), built to the village for the purposes of securing the carriage of the phosphate, runs alongside the river and the phosphate is discharged from the scows into the cars or into bins, should immediate shipment not be required. Before this branch line was constructed, the phosphate used to be carted from this point to Buckingham Basin, where it was loaded on to barges and conveyed down the Ottawa River, the rapids on the du Lièvre River between Buckingham Village and Buckingham Basin, where the du Lièvre River joins the Ottawa River, preventing water transport beyond the village.

Ascending the du Lièvre River in the steamer which plies daily between the village and High Rock landing, a point some two and a-half miles below High Falls, and 26 miles distant from Buckingham, one observes the surrounding country which is fairly flat at the start gradually change into a hillocky appearance, and at a distance of about ten miles a considerable hill, of sugar cone shape, is seen rising from the eastern bank of the river. This is the Emerald, formerly the Watt Mine, which at one time had probably the most remarkable show of phosphate ever witnessed. Mining operations were commenced on the top of this hill, about 200 feet above the river, on a small outcrop of phosphate which gradually expanded and developed until there was a chamber with walls, floor and part of the roof of absolutely solid pure apatite.

Needless to say this bonanza had its limit and in time was exhausted, but a very large quantity of pure phosphate was extracted at a very small cost. This property probably contained a greater proportion of apatite to the other accompanying minerals, and even to the country rock than any other in this region, and the veins or leads both of phosphate and pyroxene rock are most regular. The phosphate itself is dark sea-green in colour, and very hard and shiny. In part of the vein matter there is a considerable quantity of iron pyrite, which occasionally cuts right through the apatite in streaks of about an eighth of an inch in thickness. All the mining operations have been conducted by hand, no machinery or steam power having been employed. Originally the workings were made entirely from the upper surface of the mine, although the hill was most obviously suitable for the tunnelling which was afterwards undertaken.

It was on the north-east side of this hill that the Buckingham Mining Company had previously operated, and a recent visit to this part of the property showed that the apatite extracted by them had occurred in parallel leads of exceptional size, separated by walls of pyroxene rock.*

The Anglo-Continental Guano Company of London and Hamburg are now operating this part of the deposit, which is known as the Aetna Mine, and have continued the shaft originally sunk by the Company just referred to with satisfactory results. A considerable quantity of pink calcite is to

---

* NOTE.—Mr. J. Fraser Torrance, of the Canadian Geological Survey, in referring to this feature remarks: "It is perhaps worth while to note that this banded apatite and pyroxenite has never been found at a greater depth than a few feet below the soil." See "Geological Survey of Canada: Report of Progress, 1884; Apatite Reports, p. 13."

be observed in the vein matter, and the concomitant pyroxene rock is so crystallised in places that in early days many tons were mined under the impression that it was apatite.

This phosphate property is one that could have been worked (and possibly still can be) most successfully on a large scale, on proper mining principles with complete mining plant, and have yielded large quantities of mineral at a low cost. Some two years ago an attempt was made to float the Emerald Mine on the London market and provide suitable working capital, but owing to the general disfavour in which phosphate enterprises are looked upon by the English investing public, the issue did not prove a success.

Travelling a few miles further up the river, the Little Rapids are reached. At this point the river is shallow, and in the summer months much trouble is caused by the water being often so low that scows which usually carry 80 to 100 tons can only be loaded down to 25 tons, and the small steamers that do the towing cannot pass at all, so that one does the towing above this point and the other below it. The Government have been building a lock for several years, which will be ready for use next season.

About half a-mile to the east of these rapids, the Allan or Little Rapids Mine is situated. This property has been well prospected, and its richness displayed by the opening up of several good shows. A shaft has been sunk in one place to a depth of about 160 feet, and the phosphate is continuous from the surface to the bottom of the present excavations. The formation of this vein or lead is lenticular in shape, and nearly vertical in dip. The width varies from about 15 to 25 feet, and the thickness from a few inches at the surface to about 8 feet lower down. In places this bean-shaped lead goes off laterally into pockets, or separate leads.[*] The five or six acres surrounding this shaft contains an amazing number of surface shows, which may merely be small pockets, though possibly on being worked they might develop into well defined leads. The phosphate is light green in appearance, fairly hard, and very pure in quality.

The mine is fitted with a small air-compressor and with drills, but has not been worked regularly for several years, owners preferring to sell the property.

About five miles directly to the north of the Little Rapids Mine, and two and a-half miles to the east of the river, is the property known as the North Star Mine, consisting of 100 acres on the top of a hill several hundred feet above the level of the river.

This is the only mine in this district (and as far as we know in any phosphate district in Canada) which has been worked on regular mining principles. A permanent air-compressor plant was established as soon as the property had been thoroughly prospected, and a shaft sunk to a depth of 660 feet, from the study of which many false theories have been upset, and much learnt as to the occurrence, continuity and persistence

---

[*] The formation at these mines is said to have been pronounced by Professor Boyd Dawkins to be a pure fissure vein. The hanging and foot walls are well defined, and the vein has been traced for several hundred yards across the property

of Canadian apatite. Of the commercial results of the policy pursued in the sinking of this shaft we are unable to speak, but all those investors and scientists who are interested in the development of Canadian phosphate mining, owe a moral debt of gratitude to the proprietors of the property, who have thus made clear much that formerly was in doubt and dispute, proving absolutely that the beds or leads or veins of apatite are not confined to the upper parts of the formation, but extend with them into depth.

Commencing at a spot where the vein matter was only a few inches wide, the shaft was sunk to a depth of 30 feet where the vein attained a width of two feet. Continuing in depth, the vein varied from one to four feet in thickness till at eighty feet the apatite diminished into several small stringers. At 100 feet the vein expanded to one foot, and still increasing in size led to a bonanza pocket at a depth of 165 feet, and many hundreds of tons were extracted at this point at a small cost. At a point 100 feet below this the entire floors and sides were pure apatite, and drifts were run here, and at the 200 foot level into massive branches of solid ore. The same features were met with down to the 660 foot level. To sum up these results : the shaft penetrated a series of branching pockets or bonanzas of various sizes and of the utmost irregularity in their occurrence (as the ore would branch out now on the north side, now on the south in every conceivable shape), all connected with stringers or leads or narrow veins of phosphate. The apatite would also occur from time to time in quite disconnected bunches surrounded by pyroxene rock, in other parts the pyroxene and apatite would be gradually blended together. Again, at some points a section of the vein matter would show parallel but irregular veins, separated by bands of pyroxene and sharply divided from them. The dip of the vein matter is about 65°.

As would naturally be expected all the available phosphate ore was extracted as the mining proceeded in depth, but there are sufficient indications left on all sides to warrant the belief that drifts and cross levels would result in further bonanzas being developed.

A second opening about 100 feet to the east of the shaft, just described, has been sunk on an incline of about 50° following the dip of the vein matter, which has well defined gneissic walls. This pit varies in width from 20 to 100 feet, and is from 15 to about 60 or 70 feet high. Here also huge bonanza pockets have been struck, one particularly large one occurring at a distance of about 160 feet from the mouth of the pit. All the profitable ground struck was removed, and the proportion of phosphate to the total matter excavated reached a higher proportion than anything we have seen elsewhere in this district. In fact the year's working (about two seasons ago) of this pit is known to have yielded very highly profitable results.

Several other pits, in the form of open quarries, have been opened up on this property, and one particularly rich one containing a body of ore which leads into the inclined pit just described.

The phosphate bearing vein or lode is distinctly traceable over a part of the property, and various small shows have been opened up along its course.

Though all the mining operations have been conducted on sound principles, yet the question of transport to the river, a distance by road of three and a-half miles, has been sadly neglected, and all the ore has been hauled over a bad road, corduroyed or logged nearly the entire distance to the river's bank, entailing heavy expense for its transport.

Crossing now to the other side of the river, and going northwards about one mile, the Ross Mountain is seen rising abruptly from the river's bank to a height of some seven hundred feet. Stretching across from the front of this hill, on the river side, the vein matter and bands of pyroxene rock can be distinctly traced in their N.E. by S.W. course.

There are three main leads, which commence at the Ross Mountain, and traverse the country for miles, crossing the properties known as the Crown Hill, High Rock, Star Hill and Central Lake Mines. Other three leads commence some two miles higher up the river, and crossing the Ruby Lots continue into Bowman County.

Five companies have operated upon various portions of these leads, *i.e.*, the General Phosphate Corporation, Limited, on Ross Mountain ; the Canadian Phosphate Company, Limited, on Crown and Star Hills ; the Phosphate of Lime Company, Limited, on High Rock ; the Anglo-Canadian Phosphate Company, Limited, on the Ruby Lots ; and the Central Lake

Mining Company on the Central Lake Mines, with success at some points and heavy loss of money at others, according to the size of the pockets met with, and means of extraction employed.

The occurrence of the apatite is practically the same in all the mines just mentioned, and may be described as belonging to the irregular and capricious pocket formation.

In the early days of mining at High Rock, about eight or nine years ago, some enormous bonanzas were discovered and worked with great profit on the top of the hill. The original workings consisted of open quarries and cuts which were operated with a view of securing immediate returns, and the results of the years 1883 and 1884 are said to have yielded very large profits. As experience was gained, the methods improved, and an air-compressor and drills having been purchased, the work took a more permanent form. On the south-west side of the hill, some 200 feet from the top, a tunnel was run in and very rich ground struck, which has, we believe, yielded satisfactory results with astonishing regularity up to the present date.

On Star Hill the Union Company of New York commenced work in 1883, and shipped some 4,000 tons to Europe the following season, the whole average test of which exceeded 80 per cent. Their main or "big" pit seems to have been a bonanza of remarkable size, for some 9,000 tons of first quality ore were extracted in less than three years with the use of only one second-hand steam drill. In those days it was thought, and naturally enough too, that bonanza pockets were to be expected regularly, but the results of the last few years of mining have proved that these are the exceptional prizes, and that the real way to estimate the results of mining is that the proportion of apatite to be won will be in proportion to the total number of tons extracted.

What is the safe proportion on which to rely will be answered by those interested in very varying figures. In some places we have seen pits which have yielded as much as 25 per cent. of apatite from the total tonnage excavated; in others the percentage has fallen as low as a single unit. To sum up the results of our enquiries and practical work, we find that anything over 10 per cent. must be considered exceptional, and that the probable general average has hitherto been little, if anything, over 5 per cent.

Among the successful enterprises, chief mention must be made of the Blackburn Mine in the township of Templeton, about 10 miles due south of High Rock. Here the apatite is found associated with large quantities of mica, and is very pure in composition. The main working consists of a deep but narrow open pit, and the proportion of phosphate to the total tonnage extracted has always been exceptionally high. Here is found "sugar" or soft granular phosphate, friable to the touch, in considerable quantities, with mica much disseminated through it. During our last visit to this mine, some two years ago, we made a careful examination of the whole property, and traced a number of parallel courses or veins for long distances. Without going into particulars we may state that the result of our investigations convinced us that this is a property of most

exceptional merit and richness, capable of extensive development which would result in an annual output of large
quantities of first-class ore. The original proprietors worked
the mine on a small but economical scale, and the yearly
returns or profit upon the number of tons produced is said to
have exceeded the profits per ton of any other mine in Canada.

Many small undertakings have been worked in a desultory
manner in all this region, and any description of the work
would be merely a repetition of what has been already stated,
but we may mention before closing this part of the subject
several remarkable shows of phosphate which we have
personally examined.

The first was on the Stewart property, about $1\frac{1}{2}$ miles north
of the High Falls, where at the lower extremity of an abrupt
hill a few blasts had developed an extraordinary bunch of pure
green apatite. Here we measured a body of ore 35 feet in
length and 15 feet high, without a trace of a single impurity.
Thirty feet to the side was another show of nearly equal importance. Whether these shows were merely surface pockets, or
the commencement of huge bonanzas, no one could judge
without further development ; but we hear that this property,
which has since changed hands, has carried out the promises
of its initial development.

The second show was on the Murphy Lots, west of
Buckingham Village, where on a flat surface the earthy
overburden had been removed and disclosed a lead, or irregular
mass of pure ore, running for over 100 feet in length, and

varying in breadth from a few inches to several feet. We have since been informed that this was a surface-showing only, and that after the first few feet of solid ore had been removed the apatite diminished in quantity and has now lost its bonanza character.

The next show was on the west of Portland Township (W.), on what is known as the Fleming Mine. Here on the upper surface of a precipitous hill the work of a few men with picks and shovels had uncovered the most massive quantities of apatite we have ever witnessed. Some three acres of land had been roughly prospected and found to be permeated with a number of small veins of apatite about one foot in thickness, leading into the massive bunches just mentioned. At the time of our visit, sixteen months ago, we estimated that there was an available quantity of at least 3,000 tons of pure apatite which could be mined and put on carts for transport at a cost not exceeding $2.00 per ton of 80 per cent. ore. In colour the ore varied from pure green to pure red ; in places the apatite was composed of red and green crystals alternately.

Turning now to the study of the Ontario phosphate mines, the Bobs Lake Mine may be selected as fairly representing the average deposit of this section. This property is 600 acres in extent, and seems to have any number of parallel and even cross-cutting veins of pure apatite varying in thickness from a few inches to several feet. Innumerable openings have been made over this property (which has been worked by contract) and the phosphate extracted wherever found in easily worked localities.

The main opening at the time of our visit was about four to six feet wide, 20 feet long and 36 feet deep : the dip of the vein was about 70°, and the apatite had been extracted without removing any appreciable quantity of other vein matter, from which it was entirely distinct. We saw a pile estimated at 100 tons, and the quantity of refuse matter was certainly under 10 tons. The phosphate here is dark green and highly crystallised, in fact there was one pile of 20 tons, of which three-quarters, at least, were made up of hexagonal crystals. These leads appear to be true fissure veins.

On the Foxton property also there are a number of similar veins all of the same character. They occur in the country gneiss and are almost vertical, with lines of banded pyroxene on both sides. The Foxton Mining Company, Limited, started operations some years ago on this property, and the vein worked broadened out till it showed 17 feet of pure apatite, and large quantities of ore were produced at a low cost. At one time a large bowlder disturbed the vein, which was discovered again after sinking through the rock. On the Sherratt property we observed the same formation ; the ground being absolutely covered with a network of veins, which widened and diminished in turn.

At Otty Lake, one of the earliest properties mined, some of the veins have been worked to a depth of over 100 feet. In most cases the line between the vein matter and country rock is sharply defined. Sometimes the apatite occurred in regular veins, at others in large bunches, and the property is undoubtedly a valuable one.

ANALYSIS OF CANADIAN APATITE.

Having thus given a general sketch of the various undertakings, we will now consider in detail the actual working or mining of the apatite, and the methods of preparing it for market, but before doing so it will be necessary to refer to the analysis and the nature of the ore. Pure Canadian apatite tests between 88 and 93 per cent. phosphate of lime ; the following table of analyses by Dr. Christian Hoffman* gives results of selected samples :

	I.	II.	III.
Phosphoric Acid (1)	40.373 ..	41.080 ..	39.046
Fluoride (2)	3.311 ..	3.474 ..	3.791
Chlorine (3)	0.438 ..	0.260 ..	0.476
Carbonic Acid (4) ..	0.026 ..	0.370 ..	0.096
Lime	47.828 ..	49.161 ..	46.327
Calcium	3.732 ..	3.803 ..	4.258
Magnesia	0.151 ..	0.158 ..	0.548
Alumina	0.609 ..	0.705 ..	1.190
Nickel, Cobalt, and Copper	— ..	— ..	
Iron	— ..	— ..	—
Sesquioxide of Iron ..	0.151 ..	0.125 ..	1.290
Insoluble residue ..	3.890 ..	0.370 ..	3.490
Total	100.509	99.506	100.512

(1) Equal to *Tribasic Phosphate of Lime* 88.138 .. 89.682 .. 85.241
(2) Equal to Fluoride of Calcium .. 6.796 .. 7.131 .. 7.781
(3) Equal to Chloride of Calcium .. 0.685 .. 0.406 .. 0.744
(4) Equal to Carbonate of Lime .. 0.059 .. 0.840 .. 0.218

(*I.* is from Storrington, Province of Ontario ; *II.* is from Buckingham, Province of Quebec *III.* is from North Burgess, Province of Ontario).

* Geological Survey of Canada, 1879.

ANALYSIS OF CANADIAN APATITE.—*Continued.*

	IV.	V.	VI.
Phosphoric Acid (1)	41.139	40.868	40.812
Fluoride (2)	3.863	3.731	3.554
Chlorine (3)	0.220	0.428	0.040
Carbonic Acid (4)	0.223	0.105	0.518
Lime	49.335	48.475	49.102
Calcium	4.195	4.168	3.763
Magnesia	0.180	0.158	0.620
Alumina	0.566	0.835	0.565
Nickel, Cobalt, and Copper	—	—	—
Iron	—	—	—
Sesquioxide of Iron	0.094	0.905	0.125
Insoluble residue	0.060	1.150	0.630
Total	99.884	100.823	99.729

	IV.	V.	VI.
(1) Equal to *Tribasic Phosphate of Lime*	89.810	89.219	89.095
(2) Equal to Fluoride of Calcium	7.929	7.658	7.295
(3) Equal to Chloride of Calcium	0.358	0.669	0.062
(4) Equal to Carbonate of Lime	0.507	0.239	1.177

(IV. is from Portland, Province of Quebec : V. is from Loughboro', Province of Ontario : VI. is from Templeton, Province of Quebec).

The specific gravity varies from 3.130 to 3.188 and has a hardness of 5. As already mentioned the ore occurs in hexagonal crystalline masses, and even when broken up finely the same form is retained, as can be seen by the use of the microscope. At times these masses of ore are extremely hard, at others quite brittle and sometimes soft and friable. The grain of the phosphate also varies, being small and compact in some instances, while in others the granulations are large and coarse. Several remarkably large crystals have been preserved, the largest measuring 32 inches in length and 17 inches in diameter.* A still larger crystal, measuring seven feet by four feet, was uncovered at the Aetna Mine two years ago, but it was not possible to extract it in its entirety. Crystals of 12 inches in length are not uncommon, but it is always difficult to extract them unbroken.

The colour of the mineral seems to be no indication of its analysis, and many samples of red ore, usually supposed to be ferruginous, have analysed less than one per cent. of oxide of iron and alumina. When ground to a fine powder the green phosphate looks white to the eye, though the microscope reveals the green even in the smallest pieces; the red phosphate grinds to a light flesh tint.

It can be readily understood that although the analysis of samples of pure apatite runs so high, the same results cannot be expected in whole shipments, as it is not possible to separate the apatite entirely from the rocks which have to be mined at the same time and are consequently mixed in the pits with the phosphate.

PREPARATION OF THE ORE.

In the early days of the industry, shipments were sold on a guarantee of 70 per cent. minimum of phosphate of lime; later on the guarantee was raised to 75 per cent. and eventually to 80 per cent. minimum, which is now the standard minimum

* This is to be seen in the Museum at Ottawa.

of first-class Canadian phosphate. There have been instances where shipments have been even guaranteed to analyse 84 per cent. minimum, but this is quite exceptional.

The consequence of the guarantee being so low—during the infancy of the mining operations—was that not much attention was paid to the cleaning of the ore.

When it became necessary to raise the percentage, cobbing and careful hand-picking and sieving were resorted to, and at each pit there was a table or platform upon which boys broke up the mixed pieces with hammers, and selected the pure pieces. The large lumps of pure ore were set apart for first quality and the smaller pieces kept as seconds, the respective guarantees being 80 and 75 per cent. minimum. A great quantity of mixed phosphate was thrown on the dumps as useless in the years 1882-1884, since it was not thought worth while to save anything that would not analyse 70 per cent.

In 1885 the Union Company of New York leased a building and water power at Buckingham Basin, and fitted it with a Frisby-Lucop grinding mill for the purpose of utilising the "fines," or residue of the ore which passed through the screens used for cleaning the phosphate and was so mixed with small pieces of rock that separation was impossible. This product tested about 62 per cent. phosphate of lime, and was shipped in a ground state (in bags) to Buffalo and Chicago, to which points this trade is still being carried on.

About the same time improved mechanical methods of separation were introduced by the more important mines, which had now adopted regular mining machinery such as air-compressors and drills, steam drills and hoisting apparatus, pumps, &c. Large cobbing houses were erected, from the top floor of which the mine cars emptied their contents on to a sloping fixed screen made of strong bars of iron placed about two inches apart. What fell through this rough screen was shovelled into a circular wire screen, the fines from which were kept as 70 or 75 per cent. quality, and the residue as 60 per cent. and upwards.

The larger pieces of ore were passed on to the cobbing table, the pure pieces were selected and the mixed pieces broken up by hammers and then picked over.

Following the mine cars back to the loading point in or at the mouth of the pits, the details of work at the point of production have now to be investigated.

Supposing a pit to have been sunk to a point where hoisting machinery is necessary, in the form of a derrick worked either by steam or by horse, it will be understood that the work is being carried on in a space more or less confined. Holes are bored in the rock surrounding the lead of ore which is being worked, and the dynamite is fired. Before so doing the pit has been thoroughly cleaned up and the drilling machine has been either raised to the surface or sheltered in a safe position. After firing, the bottom of the pit is a mixed mass of rock and phosphate. The rock is taken out first of all, and then there remain a number of pieces of phosphate of various sizes more or less pure, mixed with the debris and small pieces of broken rock. All this has to be raised to the surface together and passed into the cobbing-house for separation. If the phosphate is hard there will be a good yield of first quality, otherwise the ore gets broken up almost into powder and inseparably mixed with the small pieces of rock. After firing the holes round a bunch of softish phosphate the interior of the pit is coated on all sides with white powdered phosphate. Much of the phosphate gets broken up by being blown against the opposite walls of a pit.

One great trouble, if not the greatest, is the changing aspect of a pit from day to day. One morning a pit will seem to be in a regular well defined vein, the next morning nothing will be seen but a few thin stringers; another dozen holes may perhaps, after firing, develop a new bonanza bunch. What is possibly still more discouraging is when there is a lead of phosphate mixed with calcite, mica and pyroxene, for though there may be no space of two feet without phosphate, yet the yield will be of ore and rock inseparably blended together, and therefore worthless except for grinding as third quality. It is this capricious "playing-out" of the phosphate that makes the results of any single pit irregular, and the only way to keep up a steady output is to have several pits running at the same time. It is, of course, impossible to predict how much dead work will have to be done when a pocket has ceased to be paying, and it is this uncertainty which causes pits to be abandoned and the machinery moved elsewhere in the hope of something better being found. Occasionally, a fault or dyke of trap rock will interrupt a good lead, but the more usual obstacle is a "horse," or large mass of country rock which has to be sunk through.

This irregularity and the absolute want of knowledge or means of acquiring any certain knowledge as to the probable future of any lead, bunch or bonanza of phosphate have helped to continue what must be admitted to be, after all, a most primitive method of conducting mining operations, for with a very few exceptions the average pit has always been worked in a way contrary to all recognised mining rules.

TRANSPORT.

The question of the transport of the ore at and from the mines has not been given, as a rule, the attention which its importance demands.

Short tramway tracks were in use at some of the mines between the pits and the cobbing houses, but the first tramway to the bank of the river was built by the Little Rapids Mine. The distance is half a mile only, and the cars which all run to the river by gravitation are hauled back by horses.

High Rock Mine was the next to improve its facilities for transport, and a rather circuitous tramway was laid from the top of the hill to the landing on the river, with a total length of about two miles. The cars are worked in the same manner here as at the mine just mentioned. From the top of the hill, where several pits were being worked, another tramway was built down to the west side of the hill to Pit XI., and the cars operated by a wire rope run by a hoisting engine.

In 1888 at the Crown Hill Mine a straight tramway was laid down the face of the hill to the river's edge, a distance of 1,000 feet, and the cars worked by a stationary hoisting engine. All the pits on this mine were connected with this point and with the main cobbing-house by tramway tracks.

These are the only transport facilities in the du Lièvre district, the other mines having to cart all their ore from the pits or cobbing-houses down the very rough roads to the river's bank. As all the mines are situated on or near the tops of hills, this work is very slow and difficult, and, as a rule, the transport has been mostly effected during the winter months, when sleighs are used instead of carts.

The ore has also to be moved on the various mines by cart to the cobbing-house, which is both laborious and expensive, and adds very considerably to the total cost. A general calculation of the cost of moving the ore on the mines from the pits to the cobbing-house, and thence to the riverside wharves, shows an average of not less than $1.50 per ton.

Transport on the du Lièvre River to Buckingham was originally done by contract ; as much as $1 per ton was paid in the early days, but this price was reduced by competition to 50 cents per ton. Some of the larger companies built their own barges or scows, and had only to pay for towage; other companies bought towing steamers as well, and did all their own transport.

To-day's expenses from the pits at the mines to the shipping point at Montreal are as follows :—

Cost of transport at mines, and thence to riverside wharves	$1.50
Loading from wharves into scows	.10
Towage to Buckingham Village	.20
Unloading scows and loading on to railroad cars	.15
Railroad freight to Montreal ..	1.25
Cartage from cars to ship's side	.25
Harbour Dues	.11
Shipping agents' commission	.25
Total cost of transport from pit's mouth to f.o.b. Montreal	$3.81

In the Templeton and Gatineau districts the minimum haulage from mines to railroad is ten miles, and in some instances the distance is considerably greater. The average cost of this transport is $2.00 per ton; railroad freight and Montreal expenses add about $1.75 to this figure.

In the Ontario mining districts, those mines which are near the Rideau Canal transport their ore to the banks of the canal, whence it is conveyed by water to Montreal.

Other mines load their ore on to the line of railroad between Sharbot Lake and Kingston, in which case the phosphate is put into barges at the latter point.

The average cost of transport from all the mines in this district to Montreal varies between $2.50 and $3.00 per ton.

LIST OF COMPANIES OPERATING IN 1891.

Name.	Mining at.	Capital.
Anglo-Canadian Phosphate Co., Ltd.	Perth, Ontario, and du Lièvre District	$500,000
Anglo-Continental Guano Works and Squaw Hill	Squaw Hill and Aetna Mines*	—
Canadian Phosphate Co., Ltd.	Star & Crown Hills*	550,000
Central Lake Mining Co.	Central Lake Mines*	—
Dominion Phosphate & Mining Co.	North Star Mine*	125,000
Dominion Phosphate Co., Ltd.	London Mine*	200,000
E. Templeton District Phosphate Mining Syndicate Ltd.	Blackburn Mine, Templeton	30,000
Foxton Mining Co., Ltd.	Foxton Mine	60,000
General Phosphate Corporation, Ltd.	High Falls* and Ross Mountain* and Templeton	750,000
Kingston Phosphate Mining Co.	Frontenac	24,000
Maclaurin Phosphate Mining Syndicate, Ltd.	Templeton	100,000
Ottawa Mining Co.	Emerald Mine*	—
Phosphate of Lime Co., Ltd.	High Rock Mine*	250,000

COST OF PRODUCTION.

It is probable that more reports have been made upon Canadian phosphate properties (and more mines offered by promoters and owners) than upon any other phosphate deposits in the world. These reports have been written by a great variety of persons, including geologists, mining engineers, phosphate experts, and owners of phosphate lands. All such reports state unhesitatingly the vast quantities of apatite which each property contains, and all agree as to the cheap cost of production, the high percentage of the phosphate, and the

* du Lièvre River District.

large profits to be made from mining the deposits. The point that all, or very nearly all, these reports are inaccurate about is just that one most essential and vital particular of the proportion of first-class ore to the total quantity of phosphate produced. We will first look into the question of cost of production of the ore, and in so doing must consider matters *ab initio*.

Supposing a property to have been roughly prospected and found to be rich in surface shows and outcrops, it is apparent that the cost of excavating the ore from such superficial pockets will not be great. In addition to this, the phosphate to be extracted can be mined without breaking it up badly, since a small quantity only of explosives is required to loosen the surface rocks. In this way it is possible to raise about 1,000 tons per annum from any fairly promising property, without any expensive machinery or plant ; but as soon as the open quarry becomes a pit, the expenses increase, as hoisting appliances, steam drills and pumps become necessary. In addition to this it is to be remarked, according to our own experience and observation, that no surface shows which contain phosphate mixed with calcite, pyroxene, &c., are selected for working, though possibly the phosphate itself may often be rusty and dirty.

In the years 1883, 1884 and 1885 the mines in the du Lièvre district were as a whole doing remarkably well and earning large profits, whereas of late years profits have materially diminished, and in several cases losses have taken their place.

This is to be accounted for in the following ways :—

(i.) When superficial pockets were being worked the mining was cheaper and the proportion of first-class quality very materially higher.

(ii.) As depth was reached more expensive machinery was required, more explosives used, and consequently the proportion of high-test quality decreased.

(iii.) Owing to the discovery of the Somme phosphate deposits, the prices realised for second and third qualities has fallen to such an extent that they do not now realise even the cost of production.

The cost of production has nearly always been stated in the various reports to be $5 per ton of apatite cobbed and ready for transport, and no doubt this figure was correct some years ago, but we have now to consider what is to-day's cost, and our estimate is as follows :—

Cost of producing one ton of phosphate at pit's mouth, in labour only	$5.00
Cost of explosives employed for same	1.00
Cost of wear and tear to plant	1.00
Cost of hand-picking, cobbing, &c.	1.00
Cost of management and sundry expenses	1.00
Total cost at mines (exclusive of transport) ..	$9.00

In the earlier days of mining in this district the second quality usually averaged about 77 per cent. of phosphate ; some years ago its grade fell to about 72 per cent., and now it is very doubtful if the average of second quality produced from the cobbing houses is over 68 per cent. This can only be accounted for by the deeper mining and the free use of explosives, which breaks the ore up into fine pieces which cannot be separated from the rock with which it is mixed.

PRICES REALISED FOR THE VARIOUS GRADES.

Year.	80 per cent.	75 per cent.	70 per cent.	60 per cent.
1882	16d. with $\frac{1}{2}$ rise	15d.	14$\frac{1}{2}$d.	—
1883	15d.	13d.	12d.	
1884	14d.	12d.	10d.	9d.
1885	14d.	11$\frac{1}{2}$d.	10d.	8d.
1886	11d.	10$\frac{1}{2}$d.	9$\frac{1}{2}$d.	9d.
1887	11$\frac{1}{4}$d.	10d.	8$\frac{1}{2}$d.	—
1888	11$\frac{1}{2}$d.	9$\frac{1}{2}$d.	8$\frac{1}{2}$d.	
1889	12$\frac{1}{2}$d.	11d.	10$\frac{1}{2}$d.	8$\frac{3}{4}$d.
1890	16$\frac{1}{2}$d.	13d.	12d.	9$\frac{1}{4}$d.
1891	14d.	10d.	9d.	8d.

These prices are ex ship London and Liverpool.

A glance at the above figures shows at once that the second and third qualities have not realised of late years prices at all in proportion to the value of the first quality.

The average value at the mines during the last two seasons of 70 and 60 per cent. qualities was about $6.00 and $3.50 respectively, showing a very serious loss upon cost of production.

If then the first quality ore has to provide for the loss upon the other two qualities before the possibility of making any profit can be arrived at, it follows that in order to make such an enterprise a success, the proportion of first-quality ore to the whole must be a high one. Unfortunately just the opposite is the case, and we doubt very much whether the first-quality ore is more than two-sevenths of the total quantity produced.

SHIPMENTS OF CANADIAN PHOSPHATE.

Year.	To Europe.	To U.S.A.	Total.
1878	3,701		3,701
1879	11,927	—	11,927
1880	7,974	—	7,974
1881	15,601	2,402	18,003
1882	17,181	2,080	19,261
1883	17,840	220	18,060
1884	22,143	32	22,175
1885	23,908	745	24,653
1886	18,972	532	19,504
1887	19,713	733	20,446
1888	14,432	2,814	17,246
1889	23,540	3,926	27,466
1890	24,154	1,903	26,057
1891	.. 14,009 ..	2,000* ..	16,009

A few hundred tons annually are also manufactured locally.

Shipments of phosphate from Montreal to Europe are not made in whole cargoes, but form the heavy ballast for stiffening the steamers. Consequently the usual amount carried by one steamer does not often exceed six hundred tons. Freights to Liverpool and London vary from 5/- to 17/6 per ton, the average being about 8/- to 10/- per ton. Should the Canadian phosphate industry assume larger proportions in the future, higher rates of freight must be calculated upon, since the quantity taken as ballast will probably not exceed about 25,000 tons annually.

PRICES OF PHOSPHATE LANDS.

In the days of mining in Ontario, the price of lands is said to have reached $300 per acre for mines situated near the Rideau Canal. Early in the last decade a very large area of

* Estimated.

lands on the du Lièvre River changed hands at a price exceeding $100,000. The purchaser was looked upon as being very foolish, until it transpired that he resold four hundred acres for $80,000 and another 1,000 for $100,000, still retaining a considerable acreage for himself. About the same time another mining property changed hands at $135,000.

Speaking generally the acreage has not affected prices, since most phosphate lands are of little or no value apart from the phosphate deposits.

About three years ago, when the demand for phosphates had become larger than the supply, and prices of phosphates of all kinds were rising rapidly, the owners of Canadian properties thought that their millennium was at hand, and London was full of promoters and property owners. The air was filled with phosphate schemes from Norway, Canada, Spain and other countries. Enormous prices were asked, and a considerable number of properties actually changed hands in different countries, and some of the more astute of the Canadians eventually realised the highest prices ever given for phosphate properties of any kind.

This brings up the question as to what is a fair value of a Canadian phosphate property, and we will venture to put our own ideas on record.

In order to arrive at a valuation the following points have to be considered :—

(i.) Possible annual out-turn and profit per annum.

(ii.) Amount of capital required to be invested for that purpose.

(iii.) Chances of getting back original cost and outlay for plant.

With these points before us, and with the full knowledge of the geological formation of these deposits and of the results of the various mining undertakings hitherto established, we say unhesitatingly that we do not know of any undeveloped phosphate property in Canada of which we could recommend the purchase at more than £5,000 as a maximum for a one-half interest, and this figure is far beyond the entire value of most of the undeveloped properties which we have explored.

Turning now to the question of developed properties, these should only be bought upon a valuation of the money spent upon plant and developments and upon the quantity or reserve of ore actually in sight, for what lies hidden is an uncertain quantity.

The most satisfactory method of operating a property would be upon a royalty of so much per ton extracted.

These are our views to-day, but it must be understood that a few years ago the position and value of Canadian phosphate properties stood upon a totally different footing. The discoveries in Florida of large quantities of high-testing phosphate, capable of being easily and cheaply mined, have altered the relative value of Canadian lands most materially ;

for whereas some years back Canada and Norway were recognised as the only countries* capable of producing high-testing phosphate, and that only in small quantities, an enormous new field with illimitable supplies has now been put into active operation.

PRESENT POSITION AND FUTURE OF THE CANADIAN PHOSPHATE INDUSTRY.

During the spring of 1890 the prices for Canadian phosphate of first quality reached the highest point they had ever touched, and it looked as if prices would go still higher. The unexpected development of high-testing phosphates in Florida at once put an end to any chances of increased prices, and the heavy shipments which came into the European market last year, and the over-abundant offers of to-day have very seriously affected the Canadian industry. Last autumn nearly all the mines suspended operations or materially reduced the number of their employés, and shipments this year are likely to be smaller than they have been for at least twelve years; in fact, last year's shipments already showed a decrease of 33 per cent.

What, then, must be done to keep the industry from dying out, and to prevent the total loss of the heavy capital invested?

*Note.—Curaçao Island, which contains deposits of high-testing phosphate, is left out of question since the owners have ceased making the large shipments received in former years.

We have shown already that the second and third qualities
do not realise high enough prices in Europe to cover cost of
production, and will now point out what is the main cause
of the general non-success of the mining operations in
Canada of late years, apart from the influence of developments
in Florida.

The present system of cobbing and of making so many
grades of ore must be discontinued. One of the heaviest
expenses in the total cost of production is in the selection,
preparation and handling of the phosphate. Instead of several
qualities there should be only two, *i.e.*, first quality of 80 per
cent. and over, and the residue which will probably average
about 62 per cent.

The proper method of operation is to select only the
absolutely pure pieces of ore in the pits, raise them to the
surface, and dispatch them direct to the bins at the river's bank
or other shipping or loading point, as the case may be.
Cobbing-houses and cobbing-boys, and double and treble
handling would thus be done away with. All the fine and
mixed ore should be kept separate and ground at Buckingham
or elsewhere, and either dispatched to points in the United
States, or else converted locally into superphosphate. If this
were done the quantity of phosphate produced and marketed
would bear a greater proportion to the total quantities of rock
mined, and would mean just the difference between profits
and losses.

As regards the manufacture of superphosphates, Canada is an immense wheat-growing country, but as yet is using only a few hundred tons of fertilisers per annum. This cannot continue, and the example of other countries must be imitated. There are extensive deposits of pyrites near Sherbrooke, Quebec Province, and others in the Province of Ontario, containing 40 to 45 per cent. of sulphur suitable for the manufacture of sulphuric acid. It therefore behoves those interested in the future of Canadian phosphate mining to digest these facts, and by the establishment of fertiliser works continue the industry and enrich their neighbours and themselves by the manufacture and sale of chemical fertilisers.

APPENDIX.

ANALYSIS OF VARIOUS PHOSPHATES.

ENGLISH PHOSPHATES.

	Cambridge Coprolites. John Hughes.		Bedford Coprolites. Alfred Sibson.
Moisture	3.13 }		2.34
Water of Combination	— }		
* Phosphoric Acid	25.20		25.40
Lime	43.33		37.22
Carbonic Acid	—		† 3.20
Oxide of Iron and Alumina			5.15
Insoluble Siliceous Matter	7.55		18.74
Undetermined		Magnesia and Alkaline Salts	7.95
			100.00
* Equivalent to Tribasic Phosphate of Lime	55.01		55.45
† Do. Carbonate of Lime			7.27

SPANISH PHOSPHATES.

	Estramadura. O. Pieper.		Estramadura. J. Hughes.
Moisture	0.23		—
Carbonate of Lime	12.27		15.22
* Phosphoric Acid	33.51		28.00
Oxide of Iron and Alumina	.91	Siliceous Matter	16.75
* Equivalent to Tribasic Phosphate of Lime	73.15		61.13

Note.—The higher qualities were practically exhausted several years ago.

ALGERIAN PHOSPHATES.

	Deckma. J. Napier.	Tarja. J. Napier.
Moisture	1.23	1.35
Organic Matter and Combined Moisture	2.95	3.10
*Phosphoric Acid ..	24.30	25.71
†Carbonic Acid	10.10	8.40
Oxide of Iron and Alumina	3.96	3.58
Insoluble Siliceous	8.75	7.40
Undetermined	7.12	9.36
*Equivalent to Tribasic Phosphate of Lime ..	53.04	56.12
†Do. Carbonate of Lime ..	22.95	19.09

FRENCH PHOSPHATES.

	Meuse. Maret.	Boulogne. Maret.	Ardennes. Shepard.	Bordeaux. J. Napier.	Bordeaux. J. Napier.
Moisture ..	1.90	4.25	—	3.27	2.96
*Phosphoric Acid	18.74	19.06	17.13	36.86	28.66
Lime..	29.23	31.92	– –	—	—
†Carbonic Acid	4.80	4.81	—	1.21	1.84
Oxide of Iron	5.46 }	4.08	—	5.60	22.25
Alumina	2.57 }				
Insoluble Siliceous Matter	28.74	27.58	34.74	2.50	3.14
Undetermined	8.56	8.30	—	2.02	1.76
	100.00	100.00			
*Equivalent to Tribasic Phosphate of Lime ..	40.90	41.61	37.39	80.47	62.56
†Do. Carbonate of Lime ..	10.90	10.93	—	2.75	4.18

SOMME (FRENCH) PHOSPHATES.

	Voelcker. 75.80	Voelcker. 70.75	Cannon & Newton. 60.65	Cannon & Newton. 55.60
Organic Matter and Water of Combination ..	1.82	.34	Moisture 2.80	2.40
*Phosphoric Acid	35.53	33.61	.. 29.10	26.22
Lime	51.81	48.15	Carbonic Acid 3.06	3.51
Oxide of Iron ..	.95	1.51 }		
Alumina	.24	1.08 }	.. 4.07	4.16
Magnesia, Carbonic Acid, &c.	9.30	12.68	Undetermined 14.10	10.45
Insoluble Siliceous Matter ..	.35	2.63	.. 8.55	15.84
	100.00	100.00		
*Equivalent to Tribasic Phosphate of Lime ..	77.56	73.37	63.53	57.25
†Do. Carbonate of Lime ..	—	—	6.95	7.97

BELGIAN PHOSPHATES.

	Mons District. Voelcker. 40.45	Liège District. Cannon & Newton. 55.60.	Liège District. Cannon & Newton. 50.55.
Moisture	.48	1.23	1.26
Organic Matter and Water of Combination ..	.68 {Carbonic Acid 3.50	3.50	
*Phosphoric Acid	18.76	.. 26.23	24.75
Lime	50.95	.. 39.04	37.12
Oxide of Iron	1.07 }		
Alumina	.77 }	3.60	4.05
Magnesia & Carbonic Acid	24.61	Undetermined and Water of Combination 6.84	6.16
Insoluble Siliceous Matter	2.68	19.36	23.16
	100.00	100.00	.. 100.00
*Equivalent to Tribasic Phosphate of Lime	40.95	.. 57.25	54.04
†Do. Carbonate of Lime	—	.. 7.95	7.95

GERMAN PHOSPHATES & NORWEGIAN APATITE.

	GERMAN PHOSPHATES.		NORWEGIAN APATITE.
	Pure sample from Statel. John Hughes.	Lower quality. Shepard.	Cannon & Newton.
Moisture	1.42	—	.. .37
Organic Matter and Water			
of Combination ..	1.90	—	.54
*Phosphoric Acid	33.45	17.56	39.92
Lime	48.18	- -	51.96
Magnesia	.65		—
Oxide of Iron	3.30)		1.14
Alumina	1.37)	—	
†Carbonic Acid	3.70	..	.. 1.36
Fluoride, Alkali, &c. ..	2.80	.. Undetermined	1.99
Insoluble Siliceous Matter	3.23	.. 35.89 ..	2.72
	100.00		100.00
*Equivalent to Tribasic			
Phosphate of Lime	73.02	.. 38.33	87.14
†Do. Carbonate of Lime	8.40	.. - -	4.09

WEST INDIAN ISLANDS.

	Navassa. Bretschneider.	Sombrero. G. H. Ogston.	Aruba. Teschemacher and Smith.	Curaçao. G. H. Gilbert.
Moisture	3.54	.. 2.57 ..	—	.. .68
Organic Matter & Water				
of Combination ..	4.64	2.90	—	.. 1.79
*Phosphoric Acid	35.60	34.22	35.40	.. 40.45
Lime	38.35	49.22	48.40	.. 51.04
Oxide of Iron ..	3.40)	1.05	2.85	.. .35
Alumina	6.50)			
†Carbonic Acid	2.58	.. 6.20 ..	11.15 ..	3.05
Insoluble Siliceous Matter	2.65	.. 1.30 ..	2.20 ..	.50
Undetermined	2.74	.. 2.54 ..	— ..	2.14
	100.00	100.00	100.00	100.00
*Equivalent to Tribasic				
Phosphate of Lime	77.71	74.70 ..	77.28 ..	88.31
†Do. Carbonate of Lime	—	14.09 ..	25.34 ..	6.93

GUANO.

	Peruvian, Nesbit.	Ichaboe.	Bolivian, Deherain.
Moisture ..	9.30	3.14	
*Organic Matter	57.30	63.52	23.00
Phosphates ..	23.05	22.20	48.60
Alkaline Salts ..	9.60	—	
Sand	0.75	1.16	—
	100.00		
*Containing Nitrogen	15.54 ..	—	4.38
Equal to Ammonia	18.87	about 13.50	4.10

	Mexillones Guano.
Moisture	10.90
Water of Combination..	11.01
*Phosphoric Acid	33.70
Lime	28.00
*Carbonic Acid	3.70
Undetermined	8.01
Insoluble Siliceous Matter	4.68
	100.00
*Equivalent to Tribasic Phosphate of Lime ..	73.45
†Do. Carbonate of Lime	8.41

www.ingramcontent.com/pod-product-compliance
Lightning Source LLC
Chambersburg PA
CBHW030323270326
41926CB00010B/1474